A *Short History of*

FOXHUNTING

A *Short History of*

FOXHUNTING

Alastair Jackson & Michael Clayton

Illustrated by Alastair Jackson

MERLIN UNWIN BOOKS

First published in Great Britain by Merlin Unwin Books, 2013
Text © Alastair Jackson and Michael Clayton, 2013
Illustrations © Alastair Jackson, 2013

Merlin Unwin Books Ltd
Palmers House
7 Corve Street
Ludlow
Shropshire SY8 1DB
www.merlinunwin.co.uk

Designed by Merlin Unwin.
Printed by Jellyfish Print Solutions

ISBN 978-1-906122-57-7

Contents

INTRODUCTION

Too many accounts of the history of foxhunting have been somewhat dry and academic. We have set out to provide a succinct account of foxhunting's history to inform and entertain newcomers and those who have hunted for years. Alastair Jackson's inimitable illustrations, born of his own long experience as a Master and huntsman, add a special dimension to our history.

The history of this great British country sport is closely linked with all other aspects of rural life. A recreation which grew out of man's ancient need to hunt, foxhunting's history is colourful and eventful. Royalty and the aristocracy have enjoyed it, but it has been highly successful as a sport appealing to the widest cross-section of society, underpinned by the staunch support of farmers and landowners throughout the British Isles. Despite profound changes, and misguided or malicious attacks, foxhunting has survived peace and war, and profound social changes.

We have described the key characters who sustained foxhunting, especially the great huntsmen and breeders who created

1

the Foxhound, in our opinion the greatest hound breed in the world. We have endeavoured to explain the science of venery with clarity. Jumping hedges on horseback in pursuit of hounds is a unique thrill, but watching hounds work in our beautiful countryside is a lifetime's preoccupation whether the foxhunter is mounted or on foot.

Foxhunting, through the planting of coverts, has made a unique visual contribution to the beauty of our landscape in many areas, and provided valuable habitats for wildlife. The pleasures of foxhunting, the beauty of horse and hound, have evoked a tradition of sporting art of which Britain can be justly proud, and a range of sporting literature which has delighted generations of readers. We have provided information and pointers for those who have yet to explore these artistic records of the hunting field.

Too often foxhunting has been grossly misrepresented by its opponents, especially those in the animal rights movement.

No history of foxhunting is complete without an informed account of the chaotic arrival of the *Hunting Act 2004*, seeking to ban traditional hunting with hounds in England and Wales.

Not least, our history of foxhunting gives full justice to the story of the fox, conserved by foxhunting as a much-valued species in our countryside. Conducted under strict rules, and observing a close season, foxhunting for so long provided a special status for the fox, conserved at an acceptable level by the Hunts. This status has been reduced to that of mere vermin by the iniquitous Hunting Act.

Despite ludicrous legislation, Britain's foxhound packs are still triumphantly in place, and making a major contribution to our way of life in the countryside. Foxhunting's heritage is that of a sport involving high skills with horse and hound, an indelible part of the rural calendar.

Youth still responds with immense enthusiasm and commitment to the appeal of foxhunting, providing eager recruits each season to the hunting field, and confounding the intentions of the prejudiced and ignorant who wished to destroy the Hunts.

Introduction

Our new, up-to-date history of foxhunting aims to inform, to entertain, and thereby to enhance a sport which for so many has become a passion and a life-long pleasure.

So in an easy-to-peruse, and hopefully entertaining manner, we're providing a concise version of how our much misunderstood, too often misrepresented, sport has survived and flourished through centuries of change in the countryside – to the benefit of the fox and its environment.

Good Hunting!

Alastair Jackson & Michael Clayton
June 2013

CHAPTER ONE

WILLIAM THE CONQUEROR AND BEFORE

After William the Conqueror crossed our shore
He felt he'd had enough of war.
So for many a year, he hunted deer
And brought the Norman venery here.

He made strict rules for voice and horn,
To be used by all who were well-born.
The poor he banned from hunting stag –
So they hunted the fox by scenting its drag.

MOST PEOPLE believe it was William the Conqueror who brought hunting with hounds to these shores and the date of 1066, when he invaded, is firmly fixed in the head of even the least attentive schoolboy. However, the English Kings before the Norman Conquest, such as Edward the Confessor, all hunted with enthusiasm and the Irish and Welsh hunted passionately, as they still do, from unrecorded ages.

However, the strongest tradition of scent hounds developed in France. St. Hubert (656-727), who hunted stag and boar in the vast forests of the Ardennes, was converted to Christianity when he saw a crucifix between the horns of the stag he was hunting. Having founded a monastery and developed his breed of black and tan hounds, he was eventually canonised as the patron saint of hunters.

The St. Hubert hounds were taken from the Ardennes into Normandy, probably in the 10th century and would have been the sort of hound brought to England by William the Conqueror. William set about preserving the forests as royal hunting grounds and put in place some savage penalties, including blinding, for killing a deer or boar, and this at a time when the murder of a man only resulted in a moderate fine. For killing a hind, King Rufus later increased the penalty to death.

These new laws to preserve game caused immense hardship and ill-feeling among the conquered Saxons, and remained a running sore in rural life for many generations. Reforms of Forest Law were part of the demands in *Magna Carta* submitted to King John. The fox, although hunted by the lower orders, was considered little more than vermin, with no protection as a beast of the chase. Indeed, suitable hounds for hunting fox or badger were apparently 'Welsh or Breton shaghaired verminers' which were particularly cunning at finding their quarry. The rough-coated hounds of Wales have survived to the present day.

The Normans produced a more defined technique for hunting with hounds, and several modern Foxhunting terms are derived from the original French. 'Tally ho' came from 'Ty a hillaut!' the huntsman's shout signalling the rousing of the deer, and 'Leu in' is another Norman derived term still widely used to encourage hounds to draw a covert. 'Leu' is a corruption of loup, the wolf. 'So-ho' was a Norman wolf hunter's cry, giving its name to London's 'saucy square mile' Soho, which was a hunting ground long before modern notoriety.

CHAPTER TWO

SLOW AND STEADY STAYS THE PACE

When fences were met by the Duke of Buckingham
His policy was for carefully ducking 'em.
'Twas the long slow hunt on a fox's drag
That pleased the field, though the pace would lag.
And ne'er they cared how the time went past
While they sat around by the earth at last –
As hounds spoke long and loudly,
While Buckingham looked on proudly.
Yet squatting for hours on the cold, bare ground
Was no good for his kidneys, I'll be bound.
The Duke caught a chill which wine couldn't kill –
So ending the life of this sporting old squire –
In a hunt where the pace was too slow to enquire.

WHEN the ruthless Norman hold on the countryside had dissipated, a passion for hunting continued for several centuries, with the management of packs of hounds being shared between royalty, the aristocracy and the local squires. Foxhunting however remained a rather steady performance, with the hounds picking up the overnight scent of the fox, known as his 'drag' and hunting slowly back to its earth. Here the hounds would sit by the hole, giving tongue melodiously while the fox was dug out.

This was the undoing of the Duke of Buckingham, the premier foxhunter in the North of England during the 1600s, who died of a chill caught while sitting on the ground waiting for a fox to be dug out. That is not to say that these early foxhunters did not achieve some long hunts. It was just that the horse, when one was used, was purely a means of following the hounds, and the challenge of crossing the country was irrelevant. Rather than use the usual 18 inch curved hunting horn of the time, Buckingham designed the small straight metal horn, which is used to this day.

Three hundred years ago West Sussex, and not Leicestershire or Gloucestershire, was regarded as the Mecca of foxhunting. It was on the South Downs that the famous Charlton Hunt was formed, probably one of the first organised Hunts to hunt the fox regularly. It was a very aristocratic affair; the list of subscribers reads like a *Burke's Peerage*: the Duke of Bolton, Duke of Devonshire, Duke of Kingston, the Earl of Pembroke, Earl of Lincoln, Earl of Sandwich….. and so on. At one time the Duke of Monmouth, the ill-fated illegitimate son of Charles II, was Master. While awaiting his execution, he wrote a letter to his huntsman, Tom Johnson, telling him which bitches to breed from! Tom Johnson died in 1744 and was buried in Singleton churchyard, near Charlton. On his tombstone is the verse:

> *Here Johnson lies, what hunter can deny*
> *Old Honest Tom the tribute of a sigh,*
> *Deaf is that ear which caught the opening sound,*
> *Dumb is the tongue that cheered the hills around.*
> *Unpleasing truth: Death hunts us from our birth;*
> *In view, then like foxes take to earth.*

The blue Charlton livery is still worn by the Chiddingfold, Leconfield and Cowdray Hunt, which covers the old Charlton country, although they do not have the gold tassels on their caps.

By now England was thronged with other packs of hounds, large and small, but the exact dates of their conversion to foxhunting is mostly unknown. Another ancient hunting establishment was the Berkeley. When Roger Berkeley was given land in Gloucestershire by William the Conqueror and Berkeley Castle was built, hounds were kept there and have been in the control of the same family ever since. Thus the Berkeleys must be considered the oldest hunting family in England.

The change from staghounds to foxhounds took place under the Mastership of the 5th Earl and the 'tawny yellow' livery of his Hunt servants was seen throughout this vast country, which stretched from Berkeley Castle on the Severn Estuary, to Berkeley Square in London. To hunt this extraordinary area, four outlying kennels were used between Berkeley and London. In 1790 the country was broken up and part of it was taken by the Old Berkeley Hunt and founded on a subscription basis; its tawny yellow coats are still worn by the Kimblewick Hunt, who hunt that country today.

Other major establishments at this time included those belonging to the Coventry family who kept hounds at Croome in Worcestershire from about 1600, the Lowthers in Westmoreland from about 1650, the Pryses in the Gogerddan country, and the Williams's in the Llangibby who both had packs of comparable antiquity in Wales.

The foxes of the Lake District were strong and expensive predators on farm stock, and must have been hunted from time immemorial. Hounds bred to hunt the Fells were first developed by Sir Thomas Cockaine in the reign of Elizabeth I and would have been 'trencher fed' (kept on the farms and brought together on a hunting day, when they were followed on foot). This method applied to some extent until recently where hounds returned to their farms in the summer, and the huntsman would take alternative farm work until they returned to the kennels for the hunting season.

CHAPTER THREE

THE HOOROOSH
OF THE CHASE

When Hugo Meynell comes to the Shires
A speedy pack he soon acquires;
Faster and faster grows the pace
'Til old Hugo's red in face.

'I haven't had a day of peace
'Since those rascals went like grease.
'Those smarty boots ride down my hounds –
'And I would give a thousand pounds
'To make rude thrusters in the Quorn
'Rue the day that they were born.'

THE 'modern' style of hunting, providing an exciting ride for the followers, dates from 1753 in Leicestershire. It was then that a young Derbyshire squire called Hugo Meynell, only 18 years old, moved his hounds and household to Quorndon Hall and hunted the country between Nottingham and Market Harborough.

This was an ideal hunting country, naturally well drained so that the grassland rode light, with well-spaced coverts that encouraged a fox to run in the open, and an undulating countryside which enabled huntsman and followers to watch hounds hunting ahead.

Meynell's early years in Leicestershire were remarkably unsuccessful because, although he had boundless energy and enthusiasm, there was no knowledgeable 'elder statesman' to help him. However, by the 1770s the Quorn under his Mastership had so improved as to be the premier pack in the land for half a century. He was a highly intelligent man, and a member of London's fashionable set – an intellectual contrast with some of the country squires depicted as Masters until then.

The Meynell method was to let hounds hunt on their own, with as little noise from whippers-in as possible. By breeding hounds for nose, pace and stamina he soon built up a pack that were second-to-none for showing sport. The performance of his hounds, combined with his personality, and the superb country over which he hunted, soon attracted a new breed of foxhunter.

In about 1780 a provincial arriviste, William Childe from Shropshire – nicknamed Flying Childe, the name given to a famous racehorse – showed how it was possible to 'ride up to hounds' by jumping the thorn fences, known as fly fences, for which Leicestershire became famous. The challenge and thrill of riding over fences at speed after hounds soon caught on, and it was not long before like-minded foxhunters were congregating at Melton Mowbray 'for the season'.

These Meltonians, as they came to be known, rode hard all day and some drank hard most of the night, getting up to all sorts of pranks. In 1837 the Marquess of Waterford and friends, under the influence of drink, daubed some of Melton Mowbray's buildings

with pots of red paint, adding the phrase 'painting the town red' to the English language.

Mr Meynell was horrified by this new breed of 'thrusters' who constantly pressed and over-rode his hounds. However, by the end of his 47 years Mastership, the Quorn had shown the way: High Leicestershire became the focus of modern foxhunting for the next 200 years.

The other establishment central to the development of modern foxhunting was that of the Duke of Beaufort in Gloucestershire. Henry Somerset was created 1st Duke of Beaufort in 1682 by Charles II; he built Badminton House, and the staghounds and harriers he established there were the forerunners of the present pack of foxhounds.

Sporting legend says that in 1762 the 5th Duke of Beaufort, at the age of 18, put his hounds into Silk Wood, a covert still existing near Tetbury, after a poor day's staghunting, and had such a good hunt on a fox that he vowed to hunt fox thereafter. In fact the general transition from stag to foxhunting was a much more gradual affair. Its cause was the progressive enclosure of the countryside. At first foxes were not very plentiful, causing the 5th Duke to extend his boundaries to take in what is now the whole of the Heythrop country. To the present day, Badminton is the traditional home of the modern foxhound.

CHAPTER FOUR

LEADING THE WAY
IN THE 19th CENTURY

Talk of horses and hounds
And the system of kennel.
Give me Leicestershire nags
And the hounds of old Meynell!

The Shires

In 1800 Hugo Meynell, ever since known as the 'Father of foxhunting', gave up the Quorn hounds after 47 seasons. He sold 50 couple of hounds and Quorndon Hall to Lord Sefton. Sefton was a very heavy man who regularly paid £1,000 for his horses, and brought the second horse system into fashion. This enabled a rider of any weight to gallop and jump all day, changing to a fresh mount brought to the hunting field by a 'second horseman' who rode quietly on the lanes until the change was needed.

Mr Thomas Assheton Smith was the first Master of the Quorn to hunt hounds himself, and was a bold enough horseman to out-thrust the thrusters.

Several important Masterships ensured the highest standards were achieved, culminating in that of Lord Lonsdale, 'the Yellow Earl' at the Cottesmore and Quorn. A consummate showman, no expense was spared and he would lay on a fleet of yellow carriages to convey his house parties to the meets.

He had inherited the immortal Tom Firr as Quorn huntsman, who, in order not to waste an ounce of his energy that might be needed in the field, would travel seated beside the Master in his yellow phaeton, while the hounds travelled in a yellow horsedrawn hound van.

The Quorn retained its reputation as the ultimate fashionable Hunt, attracting visitors, many from London, who would base themselves at Melton for the hectic winter season.

The Quorn is one of three famous Hunts around the Leicestershire market town of Melton Mowbray, sometimes called 'the capital' of foxhunting (and nowadays the venue of the Museum of Foxhunting), the others being the Belvoir and Cottesmore. 'Shires packs' are those which hunt wholly or partly in Leicestershire, and include other Hunts such as the Fernie and the Pytchley.

The Belvoir Hunt became famous as the fount of foxhound breeding in the late 19th and early 20th centuries. It derived from the family packs of deer hounds kept at Belvoir Castle by the Dukes of Rutland whose ancestor came with William the Conqueror. The pack was increasingly entered to hunt fox from about 1730 by the 3rd Duke. Earlier he ran the Hunt as a 'confederate' pack with four other neighbouring noblemen, hunting a vast country that took in much of Leicestershire, Northamptonshire, Rutland and Nottinghamshire.

In 1732 the Earl of Gainsborough left the confederacy, taking with him 25 couple of hounds and started to hunt the country known today as the Cottesmore, to the south of Melton Mowbray. Much to the anger of the Duke, he also took the cauldron that was used to cook the hounds' food, and testy correspondence still exists at Belvoir relating to the arguments over the ownership of this vessel.

Throughout the 19th century the breeding policy for the Belvoir hounds was sustained by long serving huntsmen such as Will Goodall (1842-59). He was an outstanding professional whose methods were enshrined by Lord Henry Bentick in his book *Goodall's Practice*. Goodall cleverly acquired one of the most influential stallion hounds of all time in Brocklesby Rallywood '43, immortalised in a painting by Ferneley, and described as 'the father of the foxhound of today'. He sired many litters at Belvoir; no less than 53 couple of his progeny were sent out to walk in one season.

Frank Gillard, a former whipper-in at the Belvoir, was retrieved from the Quorn in 1870 to be huntsman, and proved an excellent hound breeder as well. He bred such a level pack that only the most experienced visitors to the kennels could tell them apart. Belvoir Weathergauge '76 became the most influential stallion in the Foxhound Kennel Studbook, with four lines to the aforementioned Brocklesby Rallywood '43. The Belvoir were set to become the most influential kennel in foxhound breeding for the next few decades. Hounds remain the property of the Duke of Rutland today, although hunted as a subscription pack.

The West Country

A more provincial but no less remarkable 19th century establishment was that of Squire Farquharson in Dorset. While Peter Beckford was hunting his hounds from Steepleton and writing his classic work *Thoughts on Hunting*, he enthused the young son of his neighbour, James Farquharson of Littleton, near Blandford.

The boy, who inherited at 23, started his own pack in 1806, building kennels at Eastbury for 75 couple of hounds, stabling for 50 horses, and accommodation for the staff in the old mansion. It was from here that he hunted his 'home' country and he also built kennels at Cattistock from where he hunted the western side. For 50 years he hunted most of Dorset, including what is now the Cattistock, the Portman, the South Dorset and much of the Blackmore Vale country.

Towards the end of his long Mastership there were many complaints that he did not hunt enough the areas furthest away from kennels. It was hardly possible that he could, but he was unwilling to let anyone else take any country from him. Growing protests led to the Squire's resignation in 1856 after one of the most remarkable Masterships ever.

The North

Several northern countries remain today under the Masterships of the great landowning families who were involved in the 19th century. The Middleton kennels were built by the 8th Lord Middleton in 1858 on the family estate at Birdsall, and the current Lord Middleton remains a Master today.

The Duke of Northumberland's estates total some 80,000 acres, but the current Percy hounds did not come into the hands of the family until 1878. Lady Victoria Percy, a Master today, is the daughter of the Duke who was known affectionately in the Borders as 'the King of Northumberland', hunting hounds himself for 48 seasons. The Dukes of Buccleuch took over their hounds in 1827, and the current Duke remains a Master of this pack in the Scottish Border. His father was confined to a wheelchair following a hunting accident, but was a supportive Master for the rest of his life.

> *The Bold Buccleuch are a Northern crew –*
> *What you call a provincial pack –*
> *And they do indeed hunt near the Tweed,*
> *But nothing of style they lack,*
> *Nothing of pace or love of the chase,*
> *And the best man has plenty to do*
> *If he wishes to ride from Salenside*
> *In the lead of the Bold Buccleuch.*

CHAPTER FIVE

FOXHUNTING IN WORDS AND PICTURES

Although my verse is bad to worse,
In words and paintings the fair Chase
Has set a glorious sporting pace.
Many a foxhunter taking his ease
Enjoys the pen of Robert Surtees -
And gives more than a passing nod
To epic runs by great Nimrod.
Old England's pictured at its best
With hounds and horses full of zest –
Captured on canvas for us eternally
By artists such as old John Ferneley.

FOXHUNTING has evoked some of Britain's finest and most enduring sporting art and literature. Peter Beckford's classic *Thoughts on Hunting* has been highly praised as the first textbook on foxhunting. Beckford (1740-1811) a Dorset Squire from Steepleton, near Blandford, had his own pack of beagles at the age of 13 and, educated at Westminster and Oxford, he was a gifted linguist and learned historian. In 1779, convalescing after a bad fall, he occupied his time writing a book in the form of a series of letters of advice to a young man. A later book rivalling Beckford's is Tom Smith's *Extracts from the Diary of a Huntsman*, first published in 1838. It results from the experiences of a Master of Foxhounds hunting his own hounds in the notoriously bad scenting Craven country. The patent method of casting hounds at a check, set out in this book in the form of a diagram, is its claim to posterity. Tom Smith's 'All-Round-My-Hat cast' has remained the classic technique for a huntsman recovering the line of a hunted fox ever since.

The first quarter of the 19th century saw the birth of hunting journalism. *The Sporting Magazine* was published from 1790, earning many readers through the immense popularity of its most celebrated contributor, Charles James Apperley (1777-1843), whose pseudonym was Nimrod. He virtually invented the role of the intrepid, hard-riding hunting correspondent, reporting from the saddle. Readers in the West End and City would queue for copies of the *Sporting Magazine* to read the latest exciting instalment of 'Nimrod's Hunting Tours'. His tendency to be patronising to 'provincial' Hunts in comparison with his adoration for the Shires' infuriated some readers. Apperley was the iconic Leicestershire foxhunter, but shared the dilemma of some of his readers that he simply could not afford the sport to which he aspired. When he fell out, he declined into the role of an exiled debtor in France.

Long before that, Apperley had been cruelly reviled and lampooned by one of the 19th century's greatest novelists, Robert Smith Surtees (1803-64). Not a thrusting rider himself, but a devotee of 'purist' foxhunting, Surtees heartily disliked Leicestershire, and particularly the use of the hunting field as a means of social climbing. However, the influence of both writers on the mythology and legend of foxhunting was profound, all the more effective because of their widely different perspectives. While

Nimrod conveyed the thrills of the hunting field, Surtees magically filled in the rich tapestry of sporting England, its eccentricities, discomforts, smells, bad weather - and rascals.

Surtees reached a far wider readership throughout the 19th century and vastly entertained the literate classes with such wonderful characters as Mr Jorrocks, the sporting Cockney grocer, Soapy Sponge, the foxhunting con-man, and Facey Romford, an amateur huntsman of great ability although a rogue. John Leech brilliantly illustrated some of Surtees' novels, adding to the growing popularity of foxhunting, coaching and racing prints.

Nimrod and Surtees were to have many imitators as hunting correspondents and novelists, of varying degrees of literary abilities. G.J. Whyte-Melville (1821-78) was among the most distinguished hunting writers and poets. *The Field*'s correspondents Otho Paget (1860-1934), and Brooksby (1845-1916), pseudonym of Captain Pennell-Elmhirst, were the most effective Leicestershire correspondents at the end of the 19th century. The former was drily perceptive and not known for spending money on either his horses or his clothes – he once swapped his red coat with one he saw on a scarecrow on his way to the meet. Brooksby relied heavily on name-dropping and fervid descriptions of hectic 'quick things' across obstacles he tended to exaggerate in size and frequency.

Rousing poetry by such as Will. H. Ogilvie (1869-1963) contributed immensely to the romance and passion of foxhunting. Born in Roxburghshire, Ogilvie aged 20 emigrated to Australia and forged a reputation as a balladeer, celebrating his experiences, droving, horse-breaking and mustering in the outback. He returned to Scotland in 1901 and for the rest of his life wrote widely popular sporting verse. He produced several collected volumes illustrated by Lionel Edwards. Ogilvie's verse *Carrying On* is still relevant:

> *'There is many a threat to our sport today,*
> *But those that are threatened live long, they say;*
> *And hunting will live when its foes are gone;*
> *Sons of our sons still carrying on,*
> *Sons of their sons still riding keen*
> *To the flash of scarlet on England's green.'*

His verse *The Dusk is Down* has been quoted at many a hunting man's funeral:

> 'The count of the years is steadily growing
> The old give way to the eager young;
> Far on the hills is the horn still blowing,
> Far on the steep are the hounds still strung,
> Good men follow the good men gone;
> And hark! They're running!
> They're running on!'

Just as influential was the increasing flood of sporting art stimulated by foxhunting in the 19th century. The previous century's artists had produced paintings to grace stately homes. In Victorian England sporting prints of the chase could adorn the walls, the curtains and the dinner plates in middle-class villas, and in manor houses owned by the new landowners spawned by the industrial revolution.

In the early 1700s Wootton was painting foxhounds for their aristocratic owners, but both his horses and his hounds were based on traditional poses and lacked the accuracy of George Stubbs, who was born 42 years later in 1724. Stubbs was obsessed with equine anatomy, dissecting horses himself and making careful drawings. Having taught himself to engrave, he published *The Anatomy of the Horse* to scientific and artistic acclaim.

Stubbs remains recognised as one of the greatest English artists, and one of his most famous paintings is of the hound Brocklesby Ringwood 1788. The list of names of the 18th century sporting artists that followed Stubbs is illustrious – Sartorius, Marshall, Ferneley, Alken and Herring – several covering more than one generation of their families.

Another giant among British sporting artists, Sir Alfred Munnings (1878-1959), was the son of a Suffolk miller. His legacy includes some impressive hunting and racing scenes as well as his equestrian portraits, but many think his finest works are of landscapes, moorland ponies and gypsy scenes. A bon viveur, he enjoyed staying at length in some of the grandest houses in the land to paint commissions and perhaps not surprisingly suffered from gout for much of his life.

As president of the Royal Academy he caused a sensation at his resignation banquet in 1949, which was broadcast on the radio, by making an outspoken attack on modern art in a rambling and clearly tipsy speech when responding to the Archbishop of Canterbury and in the presence of Sir Winston Churchill (who it is understood was in full agreement with him.)

Lionel Edwards (1878-1966), perhaps the greatest 20th century hunting artist, was born the same year as Munnings, and like him, Edwards was a fine landscape painter, capturing the winter atmosphere in his hunting scenes. Having hunted all his life in a great many hunting countries, Lionel Edwards' eye for horses, hounds and country remains unequalled. Cecil Aldin (1870-1935), Peter Beigel (1913-86), who was Edwards' pupil, as was the versatile and productive John King (1929-), and more recently Daniel Crane, have all contributed enormously to the portrayal of the hunting scene – a significant element in British life which still brings immense pleasure to many.

CHAPTER SIX

THE GREAT LEAP FORWARD

Although Victoria was not amused,
Many a lady was much enthused
By the boom in chasing foxes,
Attracting gents – as well as doxies.
Fair Skittles caused the wives to mourn
When she rode out to join the Quorn.
Then, ladies of good reputations
Sought hunting's special exaltations,
Learning all the fiddle-faddle
Of wearing a habit to ride side-saddle.
And hunting's risks could not deter
When following heroes – like Tom Firr.

IN Victorian and Edwardian Britain foxhunting changed from
being a semi-private recreation to a national sport. The numbers
of people hunting increased considerably, not only in the more
fashionable countries, but also in the smaller Hunts where the sport

was within the means of a considerable section of the rural community, who were still using horses as the prime means of transport.

There were in addition plenty of farmers and villagers who had never hunted on a horse, but had a strong interest in the fortunes of their local Hunt, regarding the pack as 'our hounds'. Many non-riding farmers walked hound puppies every year, rearing them at home for entry into the pack. More country people followed the Hunt on foot or on bicycles and early photographs show huge crowds on foot attending popular meets.

The second half of the 19th century saw the rise of several exceptional huntsmen such as Will Dale (Duke of Beaufort's), Will Goodall (Pytchley) and Frank Gillard (Quorn and Belvoir). Perhaps the most outstanding was the previously mentioned Tom Firr, who was said to ride like a jockey, but looked like a judge. He arrived at the Quorn in 1872 with the experience of nine situations spread over 15 years in a variety of countries. He was fortunate when he started at the Quorn to have a vastly rich and experienced Master in Mr Coupland, a ship-owner from Cheshire.

For 27 years Firr showed brilliant sport over Leicestershire, keeping enormous fields of very well mounted followers highly entertained with deceptive ease. He perfected the technique of the 'galloping cast', handling hounds at speed -- always in front of his horse.

Tom Firr's place in the annals of hunting has been compared to that of W.G. Grace in the history of cricket, or Fred Archer in racing. For his last five years as huntsman, the ebullient and infuriating Lord Lonsdale – 'the Yellow Earl' – was Master, who spared no expense to enable Firr to show sport. However, although he rode boldly to the end, two bad falls finished his career in 1898 and he died four years later at the age of 61.

It was during this time that the Duke of Beaufort's hounds achieved their historic Greatwood Run, which lasted three and a half hours, covering 27 miles, with a furthest point of 16 miles, over three hunting countries. It was Ash Wednesday in February 1871, and the

23-year-old Marquess of Worcester, later the ninth Duke of Beaufort, was hunting hounds. The fox took them from their own country, across the V.W.H, crossing the river Thames twice, and into the Old Berks country, where he was marked to ground in a drain under the vicarage garden at Highworth. The young huntsman completed the hunt on a cob borrowed from a local farmer; hounds and remaining horses boarded a special train at Swindon, which took them back to Chippenham, the nearest station to Badminton then.

Very few ladies hunted before 1850, but numbers gradually increased, led by groups from widely different backgrounds – the aristocracy, including daughters of the great houses, and the 'professionals'.

Something of a sensation was caused by the 1876 arrival in the Shires hunting field of the beautiful and elegant Empress of Austria. She was already a brilliant horsewoman in Vienna, and came to England solely to fulfil her ambition to ride to hounds in the Shires. Accompanied by the dashing Bay Middleton, who piloted her across country, their friendship caused inevitable gossip. The Empress showed that an apparently delicate female, even a royal one, could indeed hold her place in the hunting field. Her performance encouraged many more women to accompany their menfolk to the Shires.

Foremost of the professionals, Catherine Walters, better known as Skittles, was born in Liverpool's docklands in 1839. As a child she set up the skittles in a public house, thereby earning her nickname. She learned to ride and used her beauty and strength of personality to become a top-class courtesan, becoming one of the 'pretty horse breakers' who rode and drove in London's Rotten Row. She started hunting in Leicestershire in 1860, her presence causing a huge storm of objection from some, including Lady Stamford, wife of the Master of the Quorn, but from a similar background. Skittles earned fame by remarking 'I don't know why she should give herself such airs; she's not even the head of our profession; Lady Cardigan is'.

By the turn of the century it was estimated that only about a dozen packs out of some 180 were not collecting subscriptions of some sort. Yet a significant group of aristocratic families and wealthy industrialists provided substantial financial backing for the Hunts, since the subscriptions collected left large deficits. The M.F.H., said Trollope, should be local if possible, but above all he should be rich: 'Grease to the wheels – plentiful grease to the wheels – is needed in all machinery; but I know of no machinery in which ever-running grease is so necessary as in the machinery of hunting'.

It was first thought the new railway system would be the ruination of hunting, but it had the opposite effect. An early start enabled a Londoner to be at a meet of hounds in the Midlands by 11 o'clock, and many Hunts made use of special trains to transport hounds and horses to outlying meets, waiting in a siding to return home after hunting. The Belvoir had a special railway line to the Hunt stables.

To the horror of senior hunting people, the menace of barbed wire fencing, invented in the USA, was seen for the first time in

Britain in the 1880s. It was darkly suspected some farmers and landowners used it as a mute protest when they disliked a Mastership, but it was more likely to be used as a cheaper alternative to timber or hedges which needed maintenance. The solution adopted by many Hunts was to establish Wire Funds to pay the cost of taking down barbed wire in the most favoured riding areas at the start of the hunting season, when the cattle were brought into barns, and erecting it again in the spring at no expense to the farmer.

Even at the turn of the 20th century, a major problem for hunting, seen then at least as terrible as wire, was pheasant shooting. Edward VII was passionate about the sport, which was growing in popularity. It often closed coverts to the hounds at least until the end of the shooting season at the end of January, and some gamekeepers were inclined to kill foxes to protect reared birds.

However, on the whole, foxhunters had little to fear for the health of their sport in the early years of the 20th century. Edwardian England was enjoying a period of false security before the devastation of two world wars.

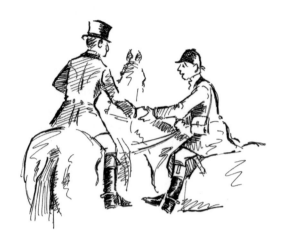

CHAPTER SEVEN

MASTERS OF THEIR SPORT

Hunting's problems came in oodles –
To be sorted out at Boodle's.
But sportsmen in this London club
Found the system quite a rub.
So off they went to meet elsewhere –
Putting their matters in repair,
And setting up a team of Masters
Who would save them from disasters?

So back in eighteen eighty one,
MFHA had then begun
To form new rules which could allow
The settlement of a hunting row.

BEFORE the mid-19th century Masters of Hounds would meet informally at Boodle's Club in St James's, London, to discuss inter-Hunt disputes over boundaries or coverts. In 1856 Lord Redesdale was made Chairman of a new Foxhunting Committee of Boodle's and for the next quarter of a century it sorted out disputes in the foxhunting world with reasonable success. The problem was that it had no power to enforce its decisions. This was made abundantly clear when the Committee tried to make a ruling on one of the most contentious hunting rows ever seen in the Midlands: Mr Coupland, the Master of the Quorn, in 1878 wished to reclaim a part of the Quorn country which had been hunted by a private pack, Mr Tailby's hounds, since 1856. He wished to resign, so the Quorn wanted the country back. It was loaned 25 years previously by a Master of the Quorn, Sir Richard Sutton, to his two sons to hunt and they passed it to Mr Tailby. The Boodles Committee upheld Mr Coupland's re-claim of this country for the Quorn, but most landowners and farmers in the disputed area did not agree.

After ten years hunted by Sir Bache Cunard the Mastership of the disputed area in South Leicestershire was taken by Mr Charles Fernie from 1888 to 1919 – and the country has remained separate as the Fernie Hunt to this day. The lesson was re-emphasised that hunting with hounds can only take place on privately-owned land with the permission and cooperation of the farmers and landowners – and no ruling body can deem otherwise.

In 1880, for reasons which are now obscure, there was a row between the management of Boodle's Club and its foxhunting members. Many of them left the club, nullifying the previous committee, and in 1881 the Duke of Beaufort called a meeting at Tattersalls, the London horse sales, to form the Masters of Foxhounds Association.

The MFHA remains the governing body of foxhunting, recognising 183 packs of foxhounds in England, Wales and Scotland, which must operate under the Association's strict rules and instructions.

Probably the most influential chairmanship of the MFHA in recent years was that of Captain Ronnie Wallace, who was at the helm for 22 years from 1970 to 1992. The two previous chairmen had been Lord Halifax and the Duke of Beaufort, whose addresses at the AGM had taken little more than a few minutes, usually summarising the sort of season it had been and perhaps exhorting Masters to ask their subscribers not to block gateways with their lorries or trailers. Suddenly, however, on the appointment of Wallace, the chairman's report would last over an hour, covering such diverse subjects as politics, the railways, badgers, the National Farmers' Union, and shooting – everything that affected hunting.

With former Master and huntsman Anthony Hart running the office, the workload of the MFHA increased greatly throughout the Wallace years, and the style of chairmanship was strongly hands-on. Nothing was neglected if it might affect the future of hunting. The MFHA is now run by a committee of 12 members, appointed on a regional basis, each serving three years, plus a Chairman, a Treasurer, professional Director and office staff.

Nowadays, apart from its powers to regulate foxhunting, the role of the MFHA has more emphasis on providing advice and education. Most advice given by the MFHA to its members is in response to telephone calls and e-mails to the office, as well as sending regular notices and instructions. While the MFHA used to only communicate with its members as Masters of Hounds, it recognises that nowadays Hunt Chairmen often take much more responsibility in the running of their Hunts.

As a result, Hunt Chairmen are included in most communications and are invited to attend the annual meeting of the Association. There are many matters which involve professional Hunt staff and require direct communication to them.

With the amount of work involved in running a Hunt under modern conditions, Masterships tend to be shorter, and a great many new Masters do not have the hunting knowledge they would have had in the past. Financial constraints mean that Hunts employ fewer staff, and there is no longer the professional ladder from second horseman, second whipper-in and first whipper-in to huntsman, which used to provide the required experience over several years in different countries. It has therefore become necessary for the MFHA

to run formalised courses for both Masters and Hunt staff. These include an annual course for new Masters, one on hound breeding and judging, a kennel management course, one for young hunt staff, as well as area meetings to update Hunt officials on how to operate under the 2004 Hunting Act, and other regulation.

The Association runs three insurance schemes, for public liability, legal fees and accidents, which are particularly geared for Hunts. It runs a Hunt Staff Jobs Registry, as well as a Bursary Scheme to train young professionals. Standards in kennels are maintained by a formal kennel inspection programme. Licences to hunt are negotiated with organisations such as the Forestry Commission, Ministry of Defence and National Trust. The MFHA is involved in the administration of Point-to-point racing, which provides a valuable source of income for many Hunts, as well as the sport of Team Chasing. The Association edits and produces the annual Foxhound Kennel Stud Book.

As the volume of work undertaken by the MFHA increased under the Wallace/Hart regime, the office, which had previously been run from the home of whoever was Secretary, moved to the Old School at Bagendon, near Cirencester, where it remained for 32 years before transferring a few miles to Daglingworth in 2008 while under the Directorship of Alastair Jackson. Now referred to as the Hunting Office, it also covers the other Hunting Associations, such as the Association of Masters of Harriers and Beagles, who have their own Director, and the smaller hound sport organisations which come under the umbrella of the Council of Hunting Associations. The Hunt Staff Benefit Society operates under the same roof.

Political work remains a priority, particularly while foxhunting has to operate under the iniquitous Hunting Act, with the modern MFHA working closely with the Countryside Alliance.

The picture of foxhunting peddled by its enemies, as an out-dated sport determinedly stuck in the past, is entirely false. It would never have survived if its ruling body had not evolved effectively to cope with the myriad complications involved in achieving our modern countryside.

Altogether foxhunting has showed a remarkable resilience in coping with the red-tape looped so tightly around our way of life since the days of Boodle's Hunting Committee. It has not survived and flourished by accident.

CHAPTER EIGHT

CHALLENGE OF THE FIRST WORLD WAR

Many a foxhunter was in the throng
As they went to war with a cheery song.
They'd be home by Christmas it was thought –
But the first Great War was so long fought.

'Mid the horrors and losses they would face,
Home thoughts in the trenches included the Chase:
A thread of scarlet across England's green,
The sweet cry of hounds – and a fox to be seen.

Too few came back from the 'war to end wars';
So many had given their lives for a cause.
For those who returned to the hunting field
There was much solace their sport could yield.

The Hunts revived and flourished anew –
Making those war-time dreams come true.

WHEN Britain and Germany went to war in August 1914, many greeted the government's decision with exhilaration, expecting a series of short, victorious battles. Patriotic Britons surged to volunteer for the forces, and foxhunting, with its strong military and equestrian connections, was in the van of the war effort. It was generally believed that some battles would be fought on horseback, and few were able to imagine the horrific implications of modern, mechanised warfare.

The Army Remount Service requisitioned over 15,000 top quality hunters in the opening weeks of war for service as Cavalry Chargers. Every kind of draught and pack animal was also in demand, and huge amounts of fodder were required from hunting countries for the expanding Army, which depended so heavily on horse power.

Hunts were rapidly denuded of subscribers, supporters, Masters and Hunt staff. Horses left in Hunt stables were on a Remount Service register, as part of the strategic reserve. It has been estimated that over 450,000 horses left Britain during the Great War and none returned, except a few officers' chargers repatriated at their owner's expense. It was possible to find ex-British Army horses, often in emaciated condition, pulling carts in Cairo's poorest slums for years after the war, and many had been top-class hunters in their day.

The Sinnington Hunt in Yorkshire was typical, with 50 farmers' sons and subscribers joining up and taking their own horses, plus ten Hunt horses provided. Both Masters –Viscount Helmsley and Mr Sherbrooke – went to war, never to return. Horses and hunting had little relevance for millions when the war developed into a horrendous slogging match, with huge armies facing each other from entrenched lines. There was massive conscription; women went to work to fill their places and food rationing and other shortages affected most households.

It was an extraordinary testament to foxhunting's firm place in rural life that it survived the Great War. Most Hunts continued with fewer hounds and horses, looked after by a much reduced staff, usually older men, some having come out of retirement. More women than ever before became Masters, hunted hounds or whipped-in. At the other end of the age scale, Stanley Barker, who was to be huntsman of the Pytchley for 30 years from 1931, was put on as second whipper-in to the Sinnington in 1915 at the age of 14, an appointment that would never have occurred in peacetime. At that age he would have been a strapper, or possibly second horseman, or kennel boy. Up to then there was a long ladder to ascend in Hunt service for an aspiring huntsman.

Feeding horses and hounds became a desperate problem, but the war government recognised hunting as a practical aid to agriculture in 'controlling vermin' and therefore resisted calls from the Food Commission to order the destruction of all hounds. However, it was decreed that hounds should not be fed oatmeal, as was the custom in those days, but only 'damaged rice and maize', and this was strictly rationed.

The hound population dropped partly through putting hounds down, but mainly by greatly reducing hound breeding. Thanks to those running the Hunt establishments, few valuable lines of foxhound breeding were irrevocably lost. Lord Lonsdale in his second term of Mastership at the Cottesmore, made a crucial contribution to carry the Hunt through the war and its aftermath. He threw himself into war work as well, and in answer to criticism that the maintenance of foxhunting was not critical to the war effort, he replied: 'What on earth are officers home from the front going to do with their time if there is no foxhunting for them?'

Military men on leave were especially welcomed out hunting, and one who snatched a day with the Cheshire when stationed near Liverpool was the author and war poet, Siegfried Sassoon. His book, *Memoirs of a Foxhunting Man*, describing his pre-war introduction to foxhunting, has become a classic, and his subsequent book, *Memoirs of an Infantry Officer*, describes his deep disillusionment with the military leadership during the Great War. After his day in 1917 his diary recorded: 'The contrast between Litherland Camp and the Cheshire Saturday country was like the difference between War and Peace, especially when, at the end of a good day, I jogged a few miles homeward with the cheery huntsman in my best pre-war style.'

His foxhunting hero and friend, Norman Loder, described in the book as Denis Milden, who hunted both the Southdown and the Atherstone before the war, was killed on active service.

It has been said that Britain lost 'the flower of a generation', and perhaps hunting suffered as much as any enterprise in losing so many young men who would have been leaders. When peace came, however, there were to be plenty of people who found themselves unexpectedly alive, with a gratuity to spend – and live life to the full. Many returned to the hunting field with a thankful heart.

CHAPTER NINE

FOXHUNTING GALLOPS ON BETWEEN THE WARS

In 'tween war years came emancipation,
And bright young things loved the sensation
Of riding bold horses o'er natural fences,
A guaranteed method of thrilling the senses.

So foxhunting prospered from the year nineteen twenty,
And offered the flappers excitement aplenty.
For the Shires still resembled an ocean of grass,
Attracting, among others, the nouveau class
Who hoped it would be just the thing
To hunt as chums of a future King.

Yet even in Hunts much in the fashion
There were still so many who hunted with passion.
Whether or not they liked social scenery –
Their ultimate aim was enjoying the venery.

41

DESPITE the initial shortage of horses and hounds, foxhunting recovered remarkably quickly following the Great War. It was to enjoy another extraordinary rise in its fortunes while the 'sea of grass' in the Midlands was still largely in place. The desperate agricultural depression of the between-the-wars years ensured that, for all the wrong reasons, there was all too much land ill-farmed, or left fallow, which produced a wilderness entirely suitable for foxhunting.

Against a background of falling trade and soaring unemployment, hunting in its traditional form managed to produce recreation for an ever widening cross-section of society in most provincial hunting countries. However, the spotlight was on the Bright Young Things who flocked back to the Shires for two decades of fashionable elitist foxhunting. There was a rather desperate gaiety for the minority able to enjoy the full social season in the 'twenties and 'thirties.

More generally, people who had no immediate family background of hunting began to take up the Chase. After the horrors of the Great War, many found the hunting field a solace from growing twentieth century pressures. Hunts had to maintain access to land, which was increasingly owned by newcomers to the country, who would be made very welcome out hunting. Farmers were rarely charged a subscription, although some would walk puppies or help the Hunt in other ways.

The hunting field swiftly reflected the growing emancipation of women and by the 1930s many of the ladies changed to riding astride. There had been major adjustments to side-saddle riding since early Victorian ladies had ridden in voluminous habits, which were all-too-likely to get caught up in the saddle in the event of a fall, often contributing to serious injuries or fatalities. Better saddles and the so-called 'safety release' riding habit skirt helped and this elegant form of riding continued to be used by some women throughout the twentieth century.

However, the emancipated flapper, who smoked and wore shorter skirts, was not so bothered by the issue of modesty. She wanted to ride across country effectively, competing with men, and chose to wear breeches and boots to use the astride saddle.

As well as more ladies riding astride, the 1920s and '30s increasingly saw the arrival of the motor car as a means of transport to the meets and some of the first motorised horse boxes to convey hunters. However, cars were still strongly discouraged from following the Hunt, although in later years car followers were to become valued supporters of foxhunting and the horse box enabled the sport to survive when some roads got too busy for horses to safely be ridden on them.

Leicestershire remained the centre of fashionable foxhunting with the Quorn, Belvoir and Cottesmore all meeting within riding distance of Melton Mowbray, from where it was possible to hunt six days a week. The country was still down to grass, with glorious fences and timber, enabling the followers to spread out and take their own line, jumping anywhere.

Edward Prince of Wales hunted from Melton, taking a suite at Craven Lodge, which had become a residential club for hunting people and their horses. He was an enthusiastic rider to hounds and relished the social life of Melton as much as the Chase. It was at Burrough Court, just south of Melton, that he met Mrs Wallace Simpson for whom he was to abdicate the throne as Edward VIII. His brothers, Prince George (Duke of Kent) and Prince Henry (Duke of Gloucester) also stayed at Craven Lodge and hunted. The much less rackety Duke of York, later King George VI, was an excellent horseman and sometimes hunted from Melton, but after his marriage to Lady Elizabeth Bowes-Lyon, they took a hunting box in the Pytchley country for several years in the 1930s, the Duke hunting with the famous Pytchley white collars over a stiff country that was arguably more formidable than the Melton terrain.

Providing and maintaining hunters, clothes and catering all helped to boost the Leicestershire rural economy at a time when farming was hard hit by the depression. Selling fodder and bedding for horses, rearing and selling hunters, were valuable adjuncts to farming in many hunting countries.

Most British foxhound packs were formed in the 18th and 19th centuries, with roots much further back. It was evidence of foxhunting's revival after the Great War that some new Hunts were born.

The College Valley Hunt in Northumberland was founded in 1924 by Sir Alfred Goodson. He remained as Master for 40 years, breeding a unique pack of Fell-Cross hounds to hunt the wild steep country of the Cheviot Hills that had previously not been considered worthy of hunting by the Duke of Buccleuch's and North Northumberland Hunts. Under the wise stewardship of the subsequent Mastership of Martin Letts, College Valley blood remains much sought-after and widely used today.

The Enfield Chace was formed in 1935, just north of London, where several of its meets could be reached by underground line or London red bus. The remaining huntable country now forms part of the Cambridgeshire. Having originally been hunted by a harrier pack, the Ashford Valley in Kent was formed in 1922 as a foxhound pack and survives to this day.

The seeds of foxhunting's postwar future were being sown throughout most of England and Wales in the 'twenties and 'thirties. One of the most significant happenings was the succession of the 10th Duke of Beaufort in 1924. As Master of the family pack of foxhounds at his ancestral home of Badminton in Gloucestershire, he was to give leadership to the foxhunting world for most of the 20th century, not least by setting high standards as a creative hound breeder and gifted huntsman.

Born in 1900, he was known as 'Master' since the age of eleven, when his father gave him a pack of harriers. His friends and relatives jokingly called the boy 'Master' and it remained a life long nickname. Hunting in the Beaufort country in the 1920s and 1930s was different from the Shires in that most of the followers were residents in the country, wearing the distinctive 'blue and buff' coats, while the Hunt staff wore the Beaufort family livery of green. Hunting was of the very highest standard, with the famous Badminton hounds the priority, becoming central to the controver-

sial changes in hound breeding in which the Duke was an important and influential figure.

There were several great huntsmen, both amateur and professional, hunting hounds between the wars. Arthur Thatcher was hunting the Fernie until 1923 and was famous for being highly criticised by Lord Lonsdale, his Master at the Cottesmore before the First War, who accused him of constantly changing foxes and of being a 'headless huntsman'. However, although he was undoubtedly a 'showman huntsman', he was hailed by nearly everyone in Leicestershire as being a huge success and he certainly caught foxes in addition to providing supremely entertaining hunting.

Frank Freeman hunted the Pytchley from 1906 to 1931 and was undoubtedly a truly great huntsman. He was a purist, a hard task master on his staff, and concentrated entirely on hunting and catching his fox. He liked racy, active hounds – unfashionable at the time – and the Duke of Beaufort wrote in his forward to Freeman's biography: 'Frank Freeman, with his pack of Pytchley bitches, and Lord Annaly as Master, were probably the greatest combination for showing sport that the foxhunting world has ever known. Their era came at the end of the Golden Age of foxhunting and set a standard that has never been, and I fear never will be, equalled again.'

On Freeman's last day as huntsman, on 4th July 1931, the Duke of York had asked that his little daughter should be introduced to hunting by the greatest huntsman. By arrangement, the Princess on her pony, led by a groom and accompanied by the Duchess on foot, waited at Boughton Covert, which Freeman drew on his way home. They found immediately and a glorious dog fox jumped over the wall bounding the covert, ran diagonally in front of the royal party, and the future Queen of England holloaed him away. Freeman jumped over the wall with his pack and, with a crash of hound music, they hit the line and hunted away.

Stanley Barker hunted the Pytchley after Freeman, from 1931 to 1960 and maintained remarkably consistent sport during a period when the Pytchley country saw enormous change from a mainly pastoral to an arable country. He exhibited great strength of character, as well as hunting skills, and served as a magistrate in later life.

George Barker, who was no relation, hunted the Quorn from 1929 to 1959 and was an outgoing personality and a very good huntsman. He had a flair for public relations, cementing a bond with the farmers and landowners with whom he was very popular.

George Tongue hunted the Belvoir for 28 years (1928–56). He was a tough man, who earned a reputation as a highly effective, disciplined huntsman. In the Great War he had been awarded the DCM for gallantry under heavy fire at Ypres. He hunted his pure English hounds in traditional style and they reacted to horn and voice swiftly, producing consistent sport across a formidable country in front of very hard riding fields.

Major 'Chetty' (pronounced 'Chatty') Hilton-Green was Master and huntsman of the Cottesmore from 1931 to 1946. It is said that he had the art of hunting his hounds correctly to catch the fox and at the same time to keep several hundred horsemen at bay. He was undoubtedly one of the very best huntsmen ever.

During the Second World War he served with the Royals and was on a ship torpedoed on the way to North Africa. He was among those rescued from the sea by a destroyer and, as he was pulled up on deck, the sailor holding the rope said, 'I thought it was about time you had your second horse, sir.' The sailor had been on the Cottesmore Hunt staff before the war.

We have already extolled the 10th Duke of Beaufort's Mastership of 60 years (1924-84), but his prowess as a huntsman for 47 years was alone remarkable enough to establish a great reputation. He was the example of a huntsman who created the pack he hunted, breeding them brilliantly to his own requirements. He knew every inch of the country, much of which he owned, and he entertained very large fields with certainty and flair, which were natural gifts.

His good friend Sir Peter Farquhar hunted the Tedworth (1927-31) while he was still in the army, the Meynell (1931-34) and Whaddon Chase (1934-38), but his vast influence as a hound breeder mainly came about during his post-war Mastership of the Portman. In those inter-war years he was an important influence among those Masters trying to improve the foxhound by the introduction of the Welsh outcross.

CHAPTER TEN

WAR AGAIN –
AND A GREATER CHALLENGE

In the decade of the nineteen-thirties
All the disciples of R.S. Surtees,
While riding keen on England's pasture,
Were heading again for national disaster.

Britain's young would face the Hun
In a struggle to be won,
To save our island from invasion,
Preserve us as a sovereign nation
Where freedom meant that British-born
Could still thrill to a hunting horn.
And once again the sport survived

When servicemen at home arrived.
It would be years away from war
When hunting would be banned by law,
Making our freedom so much littler –
A goal which had eluded Hitler.

THE Second World War was to prove a sterner test for foxhunting than the Great War, and its survival was due mainly to the farmers of Britain. More than a dozen packs ceased to operate, and all had severe difficulties surviving. Hounds were reduced to a nucleus and hundreds, carefully bred for centuries, were shot in their prime. Some breeding lines were saved by hounds being sent abroad to the USA and elsewhere.

It was fortunate for foxhunting that at last British agriculture was to be fully recognised. After the appalling depression of farming in the 1930s, when good farmland became almost valueless in many areas, the farmer was promoted high up the list of national priorities as a food producer. Farm subsidies started, and War Agricultural Committees formed in each county to step up food production.

Officially foxhunting continued because it was seen as a pest destruction exercise that the farmers deemed necessary in assisting increased stock farming, especially sheep and poultry production. Free range poultry production was the norm, and prone to fox depredation.

Cubhunting and the rest of the season were officially supposed to be conducted along the same lines, with coverts held up and as many foxes killed as possible. Inevitably foxes did run in the open, and some good sport was shown to small wartime fields, which often included servicemen and women on leave. There was no question of second horses, and many followers wore ratcatcher dress, some riding unclipped horses.

Most farmers encouraged the Masters to continue hunting and promised to help in the all-important matter of food: hay for the horses and all kinds of waste products, unfit for human consumption, for the hounds. The farmers were the only source of such food, so they held the future of foxhunting in their hands, and they made sure it survived.

The feeding of rice and Scotch oats to hounds in kennels ceased. Raw flesh was fed to hounds from fallen stock collected by Hunts from farmers as an essential part of farming practice. The Pytchley's veteran huntsman, Stanley Barker, acquired a large batch of condemned ship's biscuits of pre-1914 vintage, which fed the Pytchley hounds for about two seasons. Later, potatoes and brewers' grains were the basis of the hounds' diet and, as Barker later said, the experience shattered a few long-held beliefs on feeding; the hounds remained remarkably fit.

As in the First World War, the government immediately requisitioned many hunters for war service. The Army sent mounted cavalry regiments abroad to Palestine with some 20,000 horses, with the intention of 'maintaining a British influence' in the Middle East. Some of the military enjoyed foxhunting abroad during the phoney war with packs such as the Ramle Vale, hunting fox and jackal in Palestine. The Hon. Migs Greenall, a doyen of postwar Leicestershire hunting, was among girls working at Melton Mowbray Remount Depot during the war, breaking hunters and other riding horses to harness so that they could pull coke wagons.

The tradition of the British Cavalry and other regiments engaging in foxhunting whilst on foreign service is a very old one. The Duke of Wellington insisted that a pack of hounds, with their professional huntsman Tom Crane, were sent out to Spain as a diversion for him and his officers during the Peninsular Wars early in the nineteenth century. The strains of the hunting horn were to be heard sometimes in battle to rally troops in the Second World War, as they had been on the Western Front in the first war. Monty, before the battle of Alamein, wished his senior officers 'Good Hunting'.

The importance of foxhunting in wartime was inappropriately emphasised by the veteran Master, Lord Leconfield, who continued to hunt his own hounds from Petworth in Sussex. According to legend, during a day's hunting in 1940, his hounds checked when they encountered some young men playing a game of football on the edge of a village. His Lordship was so shocked that he stood in his stirrups and bellowed across the pitch: 'Haven't you people got anything better to do in wartime than play football?!'

Evidence that the sport not only survived the Second World War, but made a remarkable recovery immediately afterwards, is provided by *Baily's Hunting Directory's* list of packs in its 1949-50 edition, which showed an increase of ten packs since the end of the war. The fragmentation of some hunting countries into smaller areas just after the war, due to the shortage of petrol and suitable vehicles, made local hunting more convenient. Yet the increase in Hunts was equally due to more people seeking recreation in the countryside and having the opportunity to go hunting.

Up to the war many Hunts bred and maintained large packs of hounds, partly because they were likely to be decimated by outbreaks of distemper. Cuts in hound numbers during the war seemed at the time to impose damage to the breed, which would take many generations to repair. In fact, increased breeding programmes were put in hand remarkably quickly during the austerity period after the war.

No matter how helpful the farmers were to foxhunting during the war, their efforts to step up food production sharply had changed the face of rural England in a manner which seemed to threaten the nature of the sport for the future. The sea of grass, which had so attracted foxhunters to the fashionable Midlands, had receded fast, as pasture gave way to plough. The mechanisation of farming accelerated this process and some of the hedges and smaller coverts had been rooted out to increase arable crops.

On the credit side in the postwar years, the revival of British farming, receiving subsidies and guaranteed cereal prices, added prosperity and confidence to the industry, allowing farmers to be able to enjoy country sports far more. This proved a far better recipe for survival than heavy reliance on foxhunting 'carpet-baggers' from London and elsewhere. Keeping a horse on the farm for fun became far more commonplace again. Foxhunting, and indeed point-to-point racing and steeplechasing, and other horse sports all benefitted.

As always with hunting, every reverse has an upside which enables the sport to survive.

CHAPTER ELEVEN

LEADING THE FIELD
AFTER THE WAR

His fame was never jumping gates –
But he was one of hunting's greats.
Some called him god - which seemed quite odd,
Until you saw that worshipping Wallace
Gave hounds, and ladies, so much solace.

To hunt the fox the Wallace way
Became the art which many say
Was venery in its truest form?

Thus Ronnie's style became the norm
For hosts of young who hunted hounds,
Achieving sport that yet redounds
To the lessons they required
From the Master they admired.
Renowned as a modern Foxhound creator,
The Captain became a benign dictator.
As MFH Chairman for twenty-two years
He ruled supreme over all his peers.

THE HUGE impact of the war seemed in 1945 to have produced a British countryside in which foxhunting would have a much smaller position. This soon proved *not* to be the case. The wider spread of income in the post-war years, the greater mobility of people, and a surge of enthusiasm for riding, all combined to ensure that foxhunting was to achieve fresh heights of popularity in the second half of the century.

Key to the revival in postwar years were changes in the funding of Hunts, described below, which allowed some young Masters to devote themselves full-time to breeding and hunting hounds without the benefit of large private incomes.

The Duke of Beaufort, already recognised as the leading foxhunter in the land, became Chairman of the MFHA. Lord Halifax, Master of the Middleton and Foreign Secretary at the outbreak of war, once again took up the reins of this pack, which had been run by a committee during hostilities. His son, Charles Wood, had also been a Master, but was killed in action. However, his other son, Lord Irwin, now joined him in the Mastership, later to become Chairman of the MFHA and hunted the hounds himself.

Equally influential were the Barclay family, who had been Masters of the Puckeridge in Hertfordshire since 1896. At the end of the war three generations of the family were Masters – Mr Edward Barclay, Major 'Mo' Barclay, and Captain Charlie Barclay. Charlie Barclay hunted hounds himself from the war until 1987 and was pivotal in the development of post-war hunting.

Finally, the previously mentioned Capt. Ronnie Wallace (Chapter 7) became Master and huntsman of the Ludlow on their re-formation at the end of the war. He had already gained a remarkable reputation as Master of the Eton College and the Christchurch Beagles, hunting the Hawkstone Otterhounds in the summer. He was to become the most influential of all foxhunters during the latter 20th century through his 22 years as Chairman of the MFHA and long Masterships of both the Heythrop and Exmoor Foxhounds. The organisation of his own hunting country, and skills at hunting and breeding his hounds were second to none, an example many Masters tried to emulate. His interest extended far beyond his own country: his influence on the standards of hunting practice, the breeding of hounds, the careers of amateur and professional huntsmen, and the politics of the sport, was strongly felt throughout the land, and even in North America.

It became clear that foxhunting should adapt to communicating more effectively with the general public. One man, more than anyone, was responsible for persuading sometimes reluctant Masters of this during the 1950s and 1960s.

The great communicator was Dorian Williams who was born and bred to foxhunting, and was a distinguished schoolmaster, running his own adult education centre at Tring, Hertfordshire. He was a widely read author and journalist, and became nationally popular as the BBC's first TV commentator on the increasingly popular sports of showjumping and eventing. Dorian was a Joint Master of the Grafton foxhounds and later, most famously of the Whaddon Chase. Later, Raymond Brooks Ward, another equestrian TV commentator, and Master of the Enfield Chace, became professional public relations advisor to the MFHA.

At the end of an MFHA seminar on hound breeding in 1958 Dorian Williams was invited to speak on public relations, which he declared was just as important to foxhunting as it was to industry, entertainment and government, and described the right and wrong ways of dealing with the press. He recalled that he was received in polite and stony silence; only Ronnie Wallace afterwards said that he agreed with every word. Virtually every recommendation made by Dorian Williams in 1958 was to become standard procedure for the conduct of hunting from the beginning of Wallace's chairmanship of the MFHA.

Dorian Williams was responsible for encouraging the formation of Hunt Supporters' Clubs, starting the highly successful 'Whaddon Chasers' Club during his Mastership. This led to the formation of supporters' clubs in most Hunts, raising money, and acting as valuable ambassadors for foxhunting, their members coming from a wide background.

Hunt Committees found keen young men, and increasing numbers of women, willing to take on Masterships. The system of professional Hunt service revived remarkably well. Hunting countries were being organised into 'wire fund areas' with responsibility for taking down wire and building jumping places in fences. Most importantly, successful hound breeding programmes were reinstated. Horse breeding was another activity which began to boom. There was a large stock of horses in Ireland, which had been neutral during the war, and importations of excellent Irish hunters soon assisted the growth of mounted fields on the early post-war years.

Somehow funds were found during the austerity years to pay for the resurgence of hunting revival. The income increasingly came from fundraising events such as hunt balls, hunter trials, cricket matches and a host of other activities, rather than the reliance on wealthy Masters. This helped hunting to make a huge contribution to rural social life, and proved a major asset when the sport was under increasing pressure from anti-hunting factions.

Equally, in postwar Britain most Hunts had to cut back on expenses in several ways. Second whippers-in were usually only afforded by the larger Hunts, and there was more reliance on amateurs to help the huntsman. Thanks to inoculation for distemper, fewer hounds needed to be kept, and transporting horses and hounds to meets in horse boxes or cattle trucks meant fewer Hunt horses. The pre-war practice of paying an annual 'poultry fund' to those people who had allegedly lost birds to foxes was abandoned.

As farming became more intensive and land became more valuable, it was increasingly important that there was good communication between the Hunt and the farmers to ensure that hounds and horses were welcome and damage was kept to a minimum. Equally, there were increasing numbers of other interests in the country that had to be taken into account and by far the largest of these was game shooting. Near the end of the century, hunting embraced digital communication with enthusiasm, Hunts setting up their own web-sites and using email networks to communicate swiftly with their supporters and subscribers.

Organised shooting became well established during the 20th century, and some shoots restricted hunting by closing coverts to the Hunts until the end of January when pheasant shooting ceased. More often the traditional landowner would enjoy both sports, and would instruct his gamekeeper not to be too hard on the fox population. Hounds would be allowed access between shooting days, particularly in the autumn when hounds dispersed the litters of young foxes.

By the end of the century, shooting became far more commercially important on many farms and estates. Rented commercial shoots multiplied and shooting became available to many people with no other connection to the area where they enjoyed their sport. Inevitably, personal links with the Hunt grew tenuous in some districts, with shoot captains relying heavily on the advice of their professional keepers, for whom it was much easier not to have the Hunt until the shooting season was over on 1 February.

Working with the shoots became an increasingly important part of arranging hunting days for Masters. Even when access could be agreed, the number of shoots operating in an area on any particular day could make arranging a day's hunting a logistical nightmare.

As the amount of work to run a Hunt increased, Hunt Committees were finding it more difficult to engage Masters who could afford the money – and the time. The old system for a Master was that he negotiated a 'guarantee' for each season: a sum of money given to him by the Hunt Committee, who raised the cash through Hunt subscriptions, donations and fundraising events. If the Master, or Joint Masters, could not pay the full expenses required to hunt the country from the guarantee, they had to find the excess sum from their own pockets.

By the 1970s variations on the traditional system of funding Masters were brought in, and quietly encouraged by Ronnie Wallace when he took over as MFHA Chairman. Several young men with the talent to hunt hounds and who were prepared to work full time running the Hunt, were able to do so financed either by the Hunt or by Joint Masters. Most of them had gained experience hunting their school or college packs of beagles.

Meanwhile, the old system of 'open ended' guarantees was gradually shelved, with more Hunts fully financed by Hunt committees, although the Masters might well be expected to put in a fixed amount of money or provide the Hunt horses. With most Masters being busy with their own careers, it became more usual for them to share their duties between several Joint Masters.

Some of the most notable Masters of the late 20th century, who hunted and bred their own hounds, operated in a full time capacity, running their Hunts on and off the hunting field. Brian Fanshawe concluded an eminent career with a long and successful Mastership of the Cottesmore and, unlike many amateur huntsmen, he was a top-class horseman, riding many winners between the flags. Martin Scott hunted the Tiverton and the VWH, becoming a world expert on foxhound pedigrees. Michael Higgens served his apprenticeship in England before taking on the Tipperary in Ireland, where he showed fine sport for 18 seasons.

Alastair Jackson hunted both his school and college packs of beagles, and four packs of foxhounds, concluding with the Cattistock in Dorset, before becoming Director of the MFHA. His predecessor in that job, Anthony Hart, had also hunted hounds as a full time Master beforehand. Ian Farquhar left the army to become Master and huntsman of the Bicester before hunting hounds as a charismatic Master of the Duke of Beaufort's for no less than 25 years, thereafter remaining Joint Master with the Duke. Nigel Peel hunted hounds in his native Sussex and elsewhere before embarking on a long and successful term at the North Cotswold, with his wife as Joint Master, already totalling 25 years.

Some Masters managed business careers as well as giving much time to hunting, such as Stephen Lambert, who cut his teeth at the Taunton Vale, hunting two fashionable and demanding countries, the Warwickshire and the Heythrop, before becoming Chairman of the MFHA. Martin Letts ran his family diary business while hunting the College Valley hounds in Northumberland for some 40 years and remaining a Master today.

CHAPTER TWELVE

HOW THE MODERN FOXHOUND WAS CREATED

Give me the fox that holds his point though fools and fate combine,
Give me the hound that follows him with nose upon the line.
So wrote Will Ogilvie - and he was right
To stress that hounds must all be bright
In working out a line of scent
To chart which way the quarry went.
To breed for looks one has to be thorough,
And it might win fame at Peterborough.
But looks are second in every way
To a hound's real task on a hunting day.
Having a handsome pack is a perk –
But mostly you must breed for work.

OVER the years, breeding a pack of foxhounds has been the most fascinating and satisfying occupation for many men and women. There are so many points that have to be considered that are vital to a foxhound's performance in the field.

Firstly, his conformation must be such as to enable him to gallop effortlessly across country so that he can concentrate on hunting the fox rather than keeping up. He must have good scenting abilities and a voice that will proclaim it loud and clear when he is hunting the line of a fox. He must have stamina and speed and that indefinable quality of 'fox sense'. He must have the drive to press on while the fox is in front and yet must stop and turn on a sixpence when the fox has altered direction. He must 'draw' well and be willing to face thick brambles and thorns when looking for a fox.

All these vital qualities, and many more, have to be considered and brought together so that a collection of hounds will form a cohesive pack that will hunt as an effective unit. It is important that under current Hunting Act conditions, hound breeders continue to cherish these same characteristics so that, on repeal of the Act, packs of hounds will continue to perform to the same high standards as before.

It was the Norman conquerors who introduced organised hunting to Britain with their deer-hunting Talbot hounds. From 1066 to the 17th century the fox was regarded as vermin and hunting it with hounds was not considered a sport for gentlemen. When the fox was hunted, it was with the slow, deep scenting, southern hound, descended from the Talbot, which would hunt the overnight drag of the fox back to its earth.

During the 17th century a much faster type was developed in the north of England by crossing scenting hounds with some sort of coursing dogs. In Wales, the monks at Margam Abbey in Glamorgan had kept a French strain of hound given to them originally by the monastery of St Hubert in the Ardennes. These hounds were kept by the monks until the dissolution of the monasteries by Henry VIII. When these St Hubert hounds were dispersed among the Welsh Squires, they were crossed with an original rough-coated Celtic breed to produce the Welsh hound.

The strains which have produced the modern foxhound come from all of these – the Talbot, the northern hound, the slower southern hound, and the Welsh hound. Masters developed hounds that suited their own countries and, certainly up to the end of the nineteenth century, an expert could have made a pretty accurate guess as to which kennel a hound had come from.

With improvement in communications and the popularity of Peterborough Foxhound Show from 1878 (Peterborough Royal Foxhound Show from 1934), Masters were able to see hounds from the great kennels of the land competing against each other. Hound breeders became more conscious of fashion and the breed became more stereotyped.

The influence of the great family packs such as the Duke of Beaufort's, Lord Yarborough's (the Brocklesby), the Duke of Rutland's (the Belvoir), and Lord Fitzwilliam's, increased enormously and by the end of the 19th century the Belvoir in particular were considered supreme both in the field and on the flags. Bitches came from all over the land to visit the famous Belvoir doghounds that were showing great sport in their own country under huntsmen such as Frank Gillard (1870-96) and Ben Capell (1896-12).

It was perhaps unfortunate that amongst the qualities most admired in these hounds was the amount of bone that they carried, and the 'straightness' of their front legs. This led in time to a large, heavy hound that lacked activity, with exaggerated 'knuckling over' of the knees in front.

It was a professional huntsman, and among the very best there has ever been, who was one of the first to realise that things were going wrong. Frank Freeman, huntsman of the Pytchley from 1906 to 1931, steadfastly refused to breed the fashionable type, preferring a much smaller, more active sort with which he showed consistently brilliant sport across the strongly-fenced grazing grounds of Northamptonshire.

Several younger Masters hunting their own hounds between the wars were also unhappy with the popular type. They were encouraged and advised by Isaac (Ikey) Bell, who had moved from Ireland to hunt the South and West Wilts hounds. Mr Bell was a highly intelligent American with no hunting background, but with boundless enthusiasm for hounds and hunting. He was convinced the answer lay in Wales, and that by crossing English hounds with the Welsh they would obtain the activity, intelligence, nose and tongue Masters were seeking.

They found several great hound breeders in Wales who had already tried the cross, notably Sir Edward Curre, who hunted his own 'white pack' from Itton in South Wales. Such influential men as the Duke of Beaufort, Sir Ian Amory and Sir Peter Farquhar used this blood to great effect and laid the foundation for the 'modern foxhound' as we know it.

After the Second World War, Sir Peter Farquhar bred some influential stallion hounds during his Mastership of the Portman. They were widely used by many Hunts making up numbers after wartime economies. Among them was Captain Ronnie Wallace, whose own doghounds in turn were extensively used during his 25 year Mastership of the Heythrop. How often during those years were we to see 'the battle of the green coats' at Peterborough and the major hound shows, as the Duke of Beaufort's and the Heythrop stood against each other in the championships. (Huntsmen and staff in these packs wear green, the original livery of the Duke of Beaufort's.)

Although a Peterborough rosette is no criterion of prowess in the field, it was fortunate that during this time, those packs winning at shows were giving a good account of themselves on hunting days. Perhaps wrongly, many Masters are influenced by the type of hound that wins at shows and are inclined to use sires accordingly. Rather they should listen to the advice an old huntsman gave his son: 'Breed them for work and get them as good looking as you can.'

There are some other types of hound which hunt the fox to great effect, and are of use to breeders as sources of new blood or outcrosses. Several kennels still maintain the so-called 'pure English' foxhound, for example the Belvoir, Brocklesby, York and Ainsty South and County Limerick, and several others in Ireland. These hounds are mostly tan coloured and have little or no Welsh blood.

There are still plenty of packs of broken-coated Welsh hounds in Wales, and several breeders have been there more recently for an outcross. Sir Newton Rycroft, the highly intelligent and brilliant, if somewhat unorthodox, hound breeder, who was Master of the New Forest from 1962 to 1984, having experimented with French, Fell and Bloodhound crosses, came down firmly in favour of a further Welsh cross.

He bred the influential New Forest Medyg '69, who was by a pure Welsh doghound and was used by many English Masters, including the Duke of Beaufort. Sir Peter Farquhar's son Ian, who was hunting the Bicester hounds at the time, found with Sir Newton's help, a little Welsh bitch called Vale of Clettwr Fairy '73. She started another important dynasty, which then extended to Badminton when Ian Farquhar became Joint Master and huntsman there.

The Fell foxhounds, hunted on foot in the Lake District, have been developed to hunt on those steep fells, often far from their huntsman. They are light-boned and active, with wonderful voices and an independent character. In the Cheviot hills on the Scottish borders, Sir Alfred Goodson started his own pack, the College Valley, in 1924, breeding his own type of hill hound which was crossed with the Fell. These hard driving, quality hounds are still bred on the same lines and hounds of that breeding are hunted by several packs in that area.

Among the specialist packs were the Buchanan-Jardine family's black and tan Dumfriesshire hounds, which contained French blood, but were sadly disbanded in 2005. The Cotley Harriers, which traditionally hunt foxes on the Dorset, Devon borders, and have been bred by the Eames family since the reign of George III, combine the tenacious West Country Harrier blood with that of the College Valley. The unique black and tan, foxhunting Kerry Beagles, believed to have Spanish origins, have been bred by the Ryan family at Scarteen in Ireland for over 300 years.

Foxhound breeding is still a progressive science, but the final influence on how hounds perform in the field is the way they are handled. It takes much time to breed and make a pack of hounds, but a bad huntsman and noisy staff can ruin the best bred pack in no time at all.

CHAPTER THIRTEEN

FOXHUNTING THE NORTH AMERICAN WAY

If you've never been hunting with Hardaway
Then you've missed a pleasure that's hard to weigh:
A high level of venery, a great deal of fun –
And he may catch a wolf before day is done.

North American Hunts keep the accent on hound work;
Fox, coyote or possum, once found they'll not shirk.
So in the Deep South, and in east, north and west
You'll find packs of hounds all striving their best.

Apart from conducting their sport with such zest.
American sportsmen as hosts are the best.

HUNTING with hounds in North America dates back to the earliest days of British colonisation. The first importation of hounds of which there is a firm record is that by the Cavalier, Colonel Robert Brooke, fleeing England in 1650 after the Roundheads victory in the Civil War, to become 'Privy of the State within the Province of Maryland'. He arrived with his wife, eight sons, two daughters, 28 servants .... and his hounds. All his sons, and in turn their sons, kept hounds descended from his, and their bloodlines provided the basis for most of the subsequent strains of American foxhounds.

In other parts of the colony hunting with hounds began to flourish. Hounds from the Brookes' kennels came into Virginia, where the increasing number of large-scale tobacco plantations resulted in an era of unprecedented prosperity. The result was that by about 1690 there was recognisable hunting with hounds on a fair scale, wolf being the favoured quarry until its virtual extinction in that area.

The tobacco planters found the native grey fox a rather less inspiring quarry than the wolf or the English red fox which they remembered from their homeland. They arranged to import some red foxes which were liberated along Maryland's eastern shore. There were red foxes in Canada and the northern states, and they began to spread south during the 17th century, thriving on the newly-cleared land and easy pickings available near farms and villages.

Another of the earliest private packs in the Colonies was that of Lord Fairfax, who had inherited more than five million acres of land in Virginia. Arriving in 1746 to take control of his land, he hired a 16-year-old family friend named George Washington to help survey his holdings. Under Fairfax's tutelage the young Washington became a fine horseman and an avid foxhunter. As the first President of the United States of America, his favourite recreation was foxhunting. By 1767 he had established his own pack of hounds at Mount Vernon, which he kept at his own expense until just before the outbreak of the War of Independence in 1775.

In the bitterly cold winter of 1779-80 Chesapeake Bay froze, enabling red foxes to cross from Maryland to Virginia. English hounds which had been imported in earlier times were of the slow Southern breed, well-suited to hunting the native greys, but were unable to pressure and account for the red foxes. More hounds were imported from fashionable English packs, but generally lacked the tongue and lower scenting abilities needed to hunt in North America.

In 1814 two foxhounds bred by the Duke of Leeds in Northern Ireland, Mountain and Muse, were brought to Maryland, proving to be very effective fox catchers, with the necessary speed and drive lacking in the local breed. They turned out to be highly prepotent, and their bloodlines are widely dispersed across North America today through the Trigg, July and Walker breeds, particularly through the July strains found in the modern Hardaway Cross-bred. Ben Hardaway, current Master of the Midland Foxhounds in Georgia for over 60 years, has devoted his life to the development of his ideal foxhound based on the July blood of Mountain and Muse, but made more biddable through judicious outcrosses.

Throughout the 19th century foxhunting spread to the Carolinas, and west to Kentucky, Tennessee, Mississippi and Georgia, with a military Hunt from Fort Gibson in Oklahoma established in 1835. In the Deep South the phenomenon of night hunting flourished, whereby farmers and others who owned a couple of foxhounds would get together at night and sit round a fire enjoying a drink and listening to the cry of their hounds as they hunted the foxes in that area.

The Civil War ended in 1865 leaving the southern economy crippled. The planter aristocracy, formally the leaders of the foxhunting world, suffered especially. Substantial numbers of an entire generation of young Virginia men did not return from that bloody conflict, and many of the estates and plantations were inherited by women. A lack of male Masters of Hounds was to some extent filled by Englishmen emigrating to the Southern States, many of them anxious to organise foxhunting in their new country along traditional lines.

Amid the increasing wealth of the North by the turn of the 20th century, polo, racing and foxhunting were all thriving. From this background came Harry Worcester Smith, A. Henry Higginson and Henry Vaughan, who, between them, were to lay the foundations for modern foxhunting in North America.

Higginson was born into a wealthy family, but there was no way he was going to follow his father's footsteps in business and finance. Following Harvard, he dedicated his life entirely to foxhunting, living in great style as an MFH on both sides of the Atlantic and was a prolific author and collector of hunting books, now housed in the London Library. He formed his first pack in 1900 as the Middlesex Hunt Club in his home state of Massachusetts, becoming a firm advocate of the English-bred foxhound.

Harry Worcester Smith, also from Massachusetts, had always been deeply impressed by the ability of the American foxhound to pursue the red fox successfully, even on a bad scent and in the very dry conditions often experienced in North America. He formed his own pack of American hounds, which he called the Grafton after his home town, in 1904 becoming Master of the Piedmont in Virginia. As a rival of Higginson, and following lengthy debates on the qualities of their English and American packs, the high profile Great Hound Match of 1905 was arranged, consisting of two weeks hunting in the Piedmont country, which was reported daily in English and American newspapers. Although it ended in defeat for Higginson and his English hounds, it served to establish the Piedmont and neighbouring Hunts in the area of Middleburg, Virginia, as the hunting capital of the United States.

Following incursions by other packs into the Piedmont country, which could not be resolved, Smith resigned his Mastership and set about forming the Masters of Foxhounds Association of America, following a meeting at the Waldorf Astoria Hotel in New York in 1907. As secretary/treasurer, Henry Vaughan ran the MFHA from his Boston law office, travelling extensively on behalf of the Association. Later, as the most widely-respected ambassador for foxhunting, he became President of the MFHA of America.

Higginson edited the first five Foxhound Kennel Studbooks of America and remained true to his admiration for the English foxhound by refusing to register any American hounds. In fairness, it must be acknowledged that the breeding records for American hounds were incomplete and inconsistent at the time.

It is fascinating to note that when Higginson became joint Master of the Cattistock hounds in Dorset, England, with the veteran Master, the Reverend E.A. Milne, he had become a leading devotee of the Welsh cross, which horrified 'Parson' Milne, who promptly left the Mastership after only one season. Higginson remained a popular and respected Master of the Cattistock, and also took on the South Dorset during the Second World War.

In 1912 William Plunket Stewart formed Mr Stewart's Cheshire Foxhounds at Unionville, Pennsylvania, and will be remembered for his organisation for preserving and improving his hunting country. Individuals wishing to hunt with the Cheshire were encouraged to invest in a land company to buy farms as they became available in the country.

Only after re-fencing the land with post and rail timber, set well back from any roads to allow them all to be jumped, and putting in place hunting rights in perpetuity for the Cheshire hounds, were the farms put back on the market. His stepdaughter, Mrs Nancy Hannum, died in 2010, having achieved her own distinguished Mastership of that pack.

The giant among contemporary Masters in America is undoubtedly Benjamin H. Hardaway III. Ben Hardaway has bred a dominant strain of crossbred foxhounds, whose qualities are recognised worldwide. Beginning modestly in 1950, he has bred a pack which not only regularly wins at the major hound shows, but, more importantly, provides extraordinary sport in the field. Beginning with the Georgia 'July' breed, with their great drive and scenting qualities, they were however reluctant to accept discipline – a problem as the deer population increased. With the advice of the legendary Ikey Bell, who had by now retired to Ireland, Ben found the ideal cross with the Fell strain of the West Waterford and also used hounds from several English packs.

A larger than life character, who presided over one of the largest engineering companies in the country, Ben Hardaway has a sharp intellect, and is a highly entertaining companion with a fund of stories. As President of the MFHA of America, he anticipated the impending confrontation between hunting and animal rights activism and encouraged closer links with other groups, such as the United States Sportsman's Alliance.

Husband and wife Marty and Daphne Wood have both served as Presidents of the MFHA of America. They were first enthused under Ben Hardaway's tutelage, starting their own pack, the Live Oak, on the Georgia Florida borders in 1974. Since then they have spared no time or expense to develop a high class pack of English and Crossbred foxhounds, with much of the breeding influenced by their close friend, the late Ronnie Wallace. Their hounds are not only highly effective in the field, but would compete on equal terms with the very best from the top British kennels in the show ring.

Their connections with the English foxhunting world are particularly strong: they have imported hounds from the Exmoor, the Duke of Beaufort's, the Cattistock and the North Cotswold. Marty and Daphne have judged hounds at most major English hound shows; up to 2012 Marty was only the second American to have been invited to judge foxhounds at Peterborough, the first having been Henry Higginson in 1946.

In 2005, Mason Lampton, Joint Master and huntsman of the Midland Foxhounds with his father-in-law Ben Hardaway, was beginning his three year term as President of the MFHA of America. The Association's 100th anniversary occurred during his tenure and he set about organising an ambitious programme of celebratory events to promote the sport. Lampton is the grandson of Mason Houghland, founder of the Hillsboro Hounds in Tennessee. Mason's vision and skill in persuading people to contribute ensured the success of the celebrations. He used the Centennial to raise a sizable financial war chest to finance foxhunting's defence against the increasing threat by animal rights activists.

To this end he worked closely with Lt Col Dennis Foster, who had been Executive Director of the MFHA in America since 1994. With his background in military intelligence, Foster was perfectly suited to investigate and explore the deceptive agendas of organisations such as the supposedly benign Humane Society of the United States and their close links with more openly militant groups across the world. He has become the world expert on the agendas and strategies of these many animal rights – rather than animal welfare – organisations and has addressed Masters' Associations and other interested parties across the world on these dangers.

Perhaps the greatest change to hunting in North America over the last two or three decades has been the spread of the coyote population. The coyote is now the main quarry for most packs from Canada to the Southern States. As coyotes move in they tend to push the red foxes out of the area. However, the red fox still reigns supreme in the fashionable hunting states of Virginia and Maryland. Coyotes carry a strong scent and, with their size and stamina, can lope along at half speed for many hours. In order to have any chance of catching a coyote a pack of hounds must keep the pressure up and waste no

time at a check. A coyote hunt tends to be flat out. Many huntsmen like their hounds to hunt the occasional grey fox or a bobcat to make them hunt accurately, using their noses on these short-turning quarry species.

Foxhound performance trials are held on a regular basis in America, competitions usually held over two days. Competing Hunts enter their best hounds which are judged and scored by mounted judges. They hunt as one pack, following live quarry, and hunted by an invited huntsman. Each hound is clearly identified with a number painted on its side.

American summer hound shows are held in much the same way as in Britain, with classes for the various breeds of foxhound, usually including American, English, Crossbred and Penn-Marydel. Over the years, many senior judges from the United Kingdom and Ireland have been invited to judge at the American hound shows. Foxhunting has forged many friendships 'across the pond', and the sport is responsible for a very special relationship.

CHAPTER FOURTEEN

HUNTSMEN WHO LED THE WAY

Tom Firr with his galloping cast was a star,
And Thatcher was said to be nearly on par.
Then Freeman won laurels producing great runs;
All artists who earned their plaudits in tons.

Barker, Tongue, then Hilton-Green
Were huntsmen as good as any had seen.
And the twentieth century's level of sport
Was a boon for foxhunters of every sort.

Master, Duke of Beaufort, had disciples in legions
They came to be bluecoats from all other regions.
Gillson, Peaker, Durno and Wright
Were adding fresh lustre with all their might.

So foxhunting flourished despite many a change;
After the war sport was still within range.
Wallace, Fanshawe and Farquhar father and son,
Kept the tambourine rolling until day was done.

HUNTSMEN are remembered only by their reputations gained amongst those that hunted with them, but fortunately there have been some very competent hunting correspondents over the years who followed many packs and can compare the men who hunted them. During a day's hunting, the huntsman alone is responsible for the handling of the hounds and therefore gets the praise, or the blame, for the hunting that transpires.

The professional huntsman can be helped or hindered by the Master's organisation of the day, and by the control of the mounted followers achieved by the Field Master - but it is the huntsman who is inevitably remembered for the level of sport.

Hunting countries have widely different requirements; for example, a good huntsman in a wild hill country may not make a top class huntsman in the Shires. However, all the best huntsmen over the years, in whatever country they made their reputation, have been totally dedicated to their hounds and catching foxes, while still providing the sport required by their followers.

Conditions in the hunting field for the great huntsmen of the 19th century were so different from those in later years that it is not easy to compare them. The very best, such as Goodall (Belvoir 1842-59), Gillard (Belvoir 1870-96), and Tom Firr (Quorn 1872-99), are still immortalised, with Firr considered by some to have been the best huntsman ever.

In measuring modern huntsmen against the great Firr, one must bear in mind that he hunted the Quorn country when it was at its best. It was all down to grass, wire was a rarity, and the urbanisation of rural England as we know it was far away.

Firr's superb handling of his hounds was the key to his success. He gave them freedom to hunt their fox, but disciplined them to obey his voice and horn at critical moments during the Chase. His speciality was the 'galloping cast'. After the pack had made its own cast unavailingly, he would summon them with a call or a whistle, and move forward at an increasing pace, casting them widely as they fanned out in front of his horse, until they hit off the line of the fox and surged away. Galloping casts are not recommended for the average huntsman, as proved by Firr's successor, Walter Keyte. Although a fine horseman, Keyte soon sickened the morale of his hounds by long fruitless casts at the gallop over big fences. He only lasted one season. Contemporary knowledgeable opinion was that Firr was capable of providing enormous fun for the field whilst hunting the fox he had originally found within the proper limits of venery.

Arthur Thatcher, huntsman of the Fernie from 1907 to 1923, was often compared to Tom Firr. He hunted hounds with great dash and verve and was more of a 'showman huntsman', very popular with his followers and certainly caught foxes as well. Lord Lonsdale, who was his Master at the Cottesmore before he went to the Fernie, wrote him an inexcusably arrogant, but highly amusing, letter in 1904, criticising what he considered were Thatcher's hunting errors, accusing him of changing foxes too often. It was a classic dissertation on hunting hounds, whether you believe it to be fair or not, and well worth reading by anyone interested in hunting today. Ikey Bell, as a young man, hunted with Thatcher and said that sport was consistent and he was killing foxes handsomely.

After a tough apprenticeship of 17 years in countries ranging from Kent to Kildare, Frank Freeman hunted the Pytchley from 1906 to 1931, and still has a reputation as a truly great huntsman. He had a one-track mind, concentrating entirely on hunting and catching his fox. He lived with his hounds and for them, never taking a holiday for years. He was fortunate that the Master who appointed him, Lord Annaly (in office 1902-14), gave him *carte blanche* to do what he liked with the hounds on his arrival. Freeman drafted a great many and replaced them with 'nippy little bitches', whose breeding he liked.

There were many who resented this wholesale drafting of hounds and replacing them with light bitches which looked little bigger than harriers, but he was fully supported by the influential Lord Annaly. Before the end of his first season Freeman had killed all criticism by showing the best season's sport the Pytchley had seen for years, and he brought a record number of foxes to hand. Ikey Bell remembers 'those glorious Pytchley days, with the perfect combination of Master and huntsman, who each in his own sphere will never be excelled.'

George Gillson had whipped-in to Frank Freeman and reached the peak of his career as huntsman of the Warwickshire from 1935 to 1940, when the war intervened, and from 1945 to 1956. Riding at a very light weight and applying Freeman's methods with a much lighter touch, Gillson, who was loved by all, was known as the 'magical' huntsman of the Warwickshire.

Percy Durno was huntsman of the Heythrop for Lord Ashton of Hyde from 1937 to 1952, when he remained as kennel-huntsman and first whipper-in to Captain Ronnie Wallace. No Hunt servant was more loyal or more popular and, long after his retirement, Percy Durno would be seen out hunting with his beloved Heythrop hounds. His son Bruce Durno produced superb sport as huntsman of the Fernie for 31 years from 1966 to 1997. Unflappable and quiet with his hounds, as was his father, Bruce Durno slipped across country with no fuss and his hounds trusted him immensely.

Of the pre-war amateur huntsmen, the two names that stand out were 'Master' the 10th Duke of Beaufort, and Major C.C. 'Chetty' Hilton-Green. We have already discussed both men in Chapter 9. Chetty Hilton-Green will be remembered purely as a huntsman, and his extraordinary ability, in the manner of Freeman, to enable his hounds to hunt properly and catch their foxes, while keeping enormous numbers of very well mounted followers entertained across the cream of the Shires.

'Master' had the advantage of his position as the major landowner and the owner of his hounds, but he also had very large fields to satisfy. He was a purist in that he expected a hunt to have a beginning, a middle and an end. He was very critical of what he called 'mystery tours'. However, as well as being a top class amateur huntsman, he will be remembered as an imaginative hound breeder, who led the movement for the Welsh cross to improve the foxhound in the inter-war years.

The post-war years saw many particular talents emerge from the ranks of the professional huntsmen. Jack Champion, who had whipped-in to George Gillson before the war, hunted the Old Surrey and Burstow from 1947 for no less than 38 seasons. He was a fine horseman and showed it was possible to show sport in an increasingly cramped hunting country just outside London. No-one would have called him a purist, but he hunted hounds with great dash and was determined to make every day fun.

Jim Webster, possessed of a dry sense of humour, usually appeared imperturbable, with a rock-like constitution and a strong nerve, which enabled him to continue hunting the Belvoir hounds at least four days a week in this highly demanding country for 27 seasons (1956-83). He was an expert at handling these volatile pure English hounds of which he was rightly proud. His brother Clarence was huntsman of the Warwickshire for 24 years from 1958.

Albert Buckle, another huntsman of the old school, hunted the North Cotswold for four years before beginning his great partnership (1954-80) at the Whaddon Chase with Dorian Williams as a Master; it was one of the great success stories of post-war hunting. Albert was an excellent horseman and a sympathetic but firm handler of hounds. He ensured that the Whaddon Chase retained its nickname of the 'Londoners' Leicestershire', attracting large enthusiastic mounted fields.

Michael Farrin became huntsman of the Quorn at the age of only 25, having whipped-in to Jack Littleworth for five seasons previously. The brave decision of the Masters to put on such a young huntsman was proved correct and he remained at the top of his profession at the Quorn for 30 seasons (1968-98). A lightweight, impeccably turned out and a superb horseman, Farrin made crossing the Quorn country look deceptively easy. He had the ability to keep cool and think clearly while being pressed by a large mounted field, and he let his hounds really hunt without wasting a minute when necessary. It is knowing when to step in and take action at a check that marks the really good huntsman in any riding country. It is a fine line between always letting hounds have any amount of time at a check, risking being dubbed a slow huntsman, and interfering too much, which results in a pack with no concentration or 'stickability'.

Of the post-war professionals, few can have been held in higher esteem or served a Hunt longer than Sidney Bailey at the VWH. He had already hunted the VWH (Cricklade) for four seasons (1960-64) when they amalgamated with the VWH (Bathurst) and part of the negotiations stipulated that a huntsman should be found from outside. However, after two seasons there was a call for Sidney to return and he remained as huntsman of the VWH until his retirement in 2005 – a total of 43 seasons. For six seasons (1977-83) he shared the hunting of the hounds with one of the Masters, Martin Scott, who he served with complete loyalty. Although no longer a Master, Martin Scott breeds the VWH hounds with great distinction to this day.

Anthony Adams was brought up within the sound of the VWH kennels and, encouraged by Sidney Bailey, he went in to Hunt service, eventually whipping-in to Captain Ronnie Wallace at the Heythrop and then moving with him to Exmoor as his kennel-huntsman. He had completed 18 seasons in Hunt service before he became huntsman of the Warwickshire in 1982 and if the 'Wallace way' rubbed off on anyone, it would have been Anthony Adams. When he moved to the Heythrop six seasons later these methods stood him in good stead and he remained there as a popular and effective huntsman for a further 17 seasons.

Hugh Robards also whipped in to Captain Wallace at the Heythrop and became a byword for showing sport in Ireland as huntsman of the Co Limerick (1971-94) where he hunted those pure English hounds for Lord 'Toby' Daresbury. He then moved to America as Master and huntsman of the Rolling Rock.

There were a number of leading amateurs who hunted hounds between the wars, who continued afterwards, most notably 'Master' the 10th Duke of Beaufort and his good friend Sir Peter Farquhar. Sir Peter's Mastership of the Portman (1947-59) was of great influence through the hounds that he bred, and he also showed very fine sport. Sir Alfred Goodson continued to breed his predominantly white Fell cross hounds at the College Valley, later handing the horn to his grandaughter's husband, Martin Letts, who became the greatest expert on hunting a pack of hounds in a hill country and hunted the hounds himself from 1964 until 2003.

Capt. Simon Clarke was brought up in the Beaufort country where his stepfather, Major Gerald Gundry, was Joint Master. Many people considered him the very best as an amateur huntsman when he hunted the South Dorset (1962-69) and provided a notable run of good sport at the Cottesmore (1969-76). He hunted hounds with great intelligence and a natural talent, which, allied with his great abilities as a hound breeder and administrator, ensured success in these countries and later, with the Duke of Buccleuch's, the South and West Wilts and the New Forest.

Dermot Kelley, having whipped-in as an amateur to Captain Colin MacAndrew at the Zetland while he was in the army at Catterick, was an exciting talent as Master and huntsman at the Meynell (1962-75). He showed sport of a high order, attracting many visitors from Leicestershire, breeding a pack of hounds that were second to none and using New Forest Medyg '69 as an outcross. Unusually, the Meynell was Dermot Kelley's only Mastership and when he gave up he changed direction completely, forging a highly successful career for himself in the city.

However, most people would agree that the post-war history of foxhunting is dominated by one man, Captain Ronnie Wallace. As a huntsman he learned the Freeman methods through Frank's brother Will, who hunted the Eridge in Sussex where the young Wallace was brought up. In 1952 he arrived at the Heythrop, following his Masterships of his school and university beagles, the Hawkstone otterhounds and the Ludlow and Cotswold foxhounds. During his 25 year Mastership of the Heythrop nothing was left to chance – from the sale of farms and letting of shoots, to the earth-stopping and fencing – and, coupled with his remarkable talent as a huntsman and hound breeder, the result was a sustained period of sport probably unequalled anywhere for that length of time and at that standard.

His whippers-in were required to ride wide to spot foxes and to use whistles, rather than holloa, to indicate a view. Although not an outstanding horseman, the country was so well-maintained with gates, rails and bridges that he was always on hand when hounds needed him.

His Mastership of the Exmoor (1977-2002) was equally long and his methods were a formative influence on a whole school of young men who became amateur huntsmen, emulating his style of hunting hounds and his methods of hound breeding and adminis-tration.

These included Martin Scott, a hound breeding expert, who hunted the Tiverton and the VWH; Stephen Lambert, who was Master and huntsman of the Taunton Vale, Warwickshire and Heythrop, before becoming Chairman of the MFHA; Alastair Jackson, who was Master and huntsman of the West Percy, South Dorset, Grafton and Cattistock, before becoming Director of the MFHA; and Edward Lycett-Green at the York and Ainsty (South), Ludlow, Portman and Golden Valley. Nigel Peel hunted the Goath-land and Cambridgeshire before his eleven seasons at the Chidding-fold, Leconfield and Cowdray, and currently in his 25th season at the North Cotswold, where he has bred an exceptionally quality pack.

Brian Fanshawe and his cousin Ian Farquhar were never of the Wallace school. Both their fathers had hunted hounds and each

had a natural talent, both as huntsmen and horsemen, with highly effective individual styles of hunting hounds. Brian Fanshawe had hunted the Warwickshire, the Galway Blazers and the North Cotswold before his highly successful Mastership of the Cottesmore (1981-91), which he ran with firm, expert leadership and showed exceptional sport.

Captain Ian Farquhar, Sir Peter's son, has had two long and distinguished Masterships at the Bicester (1973-85) and the Duke of Beaufort's (1985-), where he remains a Master, having hunted the hounds himself for 27 years. Ian Farquhar has a quiet style of hunting hounds, but like all good huntsmen, he knows exactly when to let hounds solve a problem themselves and when he must pick them up and cast them. There is a great spirit in the Beaufort country and this is largely due to Ian's leadership.

It is remarkable that under the problems caused by the Hunting Act, there are still good young men willing to take up the challenges of hunting hounds as a Master. The two of the younger generation who stand out from their peers are Richard Tyacke at the Wynnstay and Charles Frampton at the Heythrop.

CHAPTER 15

THE MYSTERIOUS REYNARD

The fox is a creature of mystery and guile
Who keeps humans guessing while living in style.
His out-of-town diet may be poultry or lambs,
But in cities, for grub, into dustbins he crams.

His tribe had its dark side, like suffering from rabies -
And lately dear Reynard's been caught biting babies.

Reynard's best when residing in coverts,
Where dog foxes roam in search of new lovers.
The status was highest for all of his race
When hunted by hounds in the glorious Chase.

There were rules, and due care, when hound work was legal;
The fox's rank in the land was regarded near regal.

Charles James was granted a summertime lull
Before hunting engaged in a minimal cull.
If hounds caught the fox his death was a rush,
But many a time he escaped with his brush.

Since Labour enacted its ridiculous 'ban',
Reynard's just vermin – the enemy of man.

THE FOX (*vulpes vulpes*) is a fabled creature. It has figured in man's history ever since it was recorded, but the origin of the species is pre-Ice Age, and it has proved amazingly adaptable. Neolithic man is believed to have eaten foxes – contradicting Oscar Wilde's famous remark that foxhunting is 'the unspeakable in full pursuit of the uneatable.'

It is often forgotten that Wilde made this witticism in a speech after a hunting dinner, and was applauded by amused foxhunters.

For centuries the fox was killed throughout Europe as a pest raiding lambs and poultry. Under its tail, called a 'brush' by foxhunters, the fox has a scent gland which produces droplets of scent which are detected by hounds with widely varying success, depending heavily on ground and air temperatures, wind strengths, and other factors which remain something of a mystery.

The fox is notably susceptible to rabies, a risk to other mammals in many countries. It was said to be due to the spread of rabies in pre-war Europe that Hitler's Germany became the first European country to ban hunting with hounds to help avoid the disease. Goering was concerned that it might interfere with his game shooting.

In post-war Europe some other countries, including Belgium and Holland, banned hunting with hounds for similar reasons, but the French claimed to have halted the spread of rabies from the east after the war through using vaccine on bait dropped for foxes and other wild mammals. The French continue to hunt with hounds legally for deer, boar, foxes and hares, rabbits and badgers.

In North America all foxhounds are vaccinated against rabies which occurs sporadically and widely in American wildlife. Britain's tight quarantine rules for imported canines protected us from rabies becoming endemic in our wildlife. Hunting with hounds would have been banned immediately if this had occurred, but a case of rabies in foxes has long been feared.

Control of foxes in the UK countryside is exercised by gamekeepers and some farmers shooting and snaring as many as possible to protect game birds reared for the growing sport of shooting. Foxes will kill young reared game, although experienced hunting people believe this risk does not justify draconian attempts by some gamekeepers to exterminate *all* foxes in their district. The

MFHA and shooting organizations preached mutual cooperation, with a give-and-take attitude to preserving fox populations. But this virtually ended when Labour's legal ban on hunting with hounds, the *Hunting Act 2004* became law on 18 February 2005, thereby endangering the fox in the countryside far more than previously when hunting them with hounds was legal.

After the decline of deer hunting, due to major reduction in Britain's forests, the rise of foxhunting with hounds in England in the late 18th and early 19th centuries gave the fox a special status. It was a prized quarry culled by packs of foxhounds for sport, with the aim of conserving the species at a level acceptable to local farming. The fox lost this historic status when the Hunting Act was enacted (see Chapter 16).

As explained by distinguished veterinary surgeons in the Veterinary Association for Wildlife Management, and the Middle Way Group in Parliament (see Chapter 16): 'The aim of wildlife management is crucially different from pest control. In the latter it is the elimination of the target species that is the motive, frequently using unnatural methods that can cause high degrees of suffering. Management has the aim of seeking to reach acceptable and sustainable levels of wildlife populations. Hunting with hounds, and those many unpaid 'eyes and ears' of its supporters, are a valuable and natural component of the management process.'

From the early 19th century onwards it was considered 'bad form', and even a cause for social disgrace, if a landowner was known to kill the foxes in his covert, so that they were blank when the local Hunt called. You will find references to this in literature by Trollope and other Victorian writers.

The fox's fate in the countryside since the Hunting Act has been far less protected. Not only gamekeepers but some members of shoots will bang away at a fox with their shotguns if they see one during a shooting day.

The wolf has long been exterminated as a threat to farm stock in Britain, but the British fox survived as an accepted part of our wild-life solely because of the notable popularity of foxhunting in the past 250 to 300 years.

It is perfectly possible to love the fox, as well as to hunt him. R.S. Surtees expressed this in the words of his immortal hunting grocer, Mr Jorrocks: '…it aren't that I loves the fox less, but I loves the 'ound more.'

Beautiful, lithe, yet a ruthless and cunning hunter, the fox has long been reviled – and admired. Foxes mate from late December to February. Gestation is about 52 days, and cubs are born mainly in March and April, usually in litters of three to seven. A dog fox and vixen will both assist in parenting, although sometimes foxes live in groups of one adult male and several vixens; one or two vixens in the group breeds, and the other vixens will assist in providing food. Hunts were appreciated by farmers in dispersing foxes as well as culling them, thereby reducing the risk to lambs and hens.

Foxes will live snug and dry underground in 'earths' for much of the year; in hill countries they may dwell among rocks. Usually in summer most foxes live above ground continuously, and a few will do so all the year round, known as 'stub' foxes.

Estimates of the British fox population are unreliable, but in 2004 it was put at around 220,000 before the breeding season, and naturalists have said the population trebles by early summer. The fox has no natural predator, so man carries out a cull. In 2013 the adult rural fox population was estimated at 225,000 with another 33,000 living in the towns. More foxes migrated to the suburbs and inner cities because the Hunting Act led to increased all-year-round fox control with guns and snares in the countryside. In February 2013 there was public alarm when a fox savaged a baby in its bedroom in South London, following other sporadic attacks on children in urban areas. Sentimentalists feeding foxes in their gardens were blamed for encouraging foxes to enter houses.

The Masters of Foxhounds Association said that before 2005 the 185 registered Foxhunts killed about 15,000 to 16,000 foxes per year, and others were killed by the gunpacks operating in Wales using hounds to flush foxes from coverts to be shot when they emerge, a process involving a risk of wounding rather than killing the fox outright.

Gamekeepers were estimated to have shot and snared at least 150,000 foxes annually before the Hunting Act, and this is believed to have increased since. Countless foxes are killed or grievously injured daily by traffic on UK roads and lanes, and freelance vermin killers account for more by unmonitored, and illegal use of terriers and spade-work.

According to naturalists foxes have such resilience that populations can withstand up to 75 percent mortality without annihilation.

The purported reason for banning hunting with hounds, alleged by animal rights groups, was that 'unacceptable suffering' was caused to the fox while being pursued by hounds, and its death if caught by the hounds.

But according to the Veterinary Association for Wildlife Management: 'There is no scientific evidence that foxes or any of the quarry species, suffer irreversible physiological or pathological damage as a result of being chased... when hunted by hounds in its own territory, and in an environment that it knows, the fox is in control... both wild and domestic animals are at their most stressed when harassed in an environment that is strange to them... they do not appear to have any premonition of death.'

Before the Hunting Act about half of all foxes killed by hounds were dispatched by Hunts in the 'autumn hunting' period when the aim was not to hunt the fox across country, but to catch it in covert. Hounds tended to catch the weaker or older quarry, and this was a genuine contribution to the conservation of the species at its best.

Anti-hunters dwelt heavily in propaganda on the horrors of being 'torn to pieces' by hounds, but when a fox is caught by hounds they kill it immediately; the animal is not left to die slowly in agony, which cannot be claimed by other means of control widely used. If it is not caught by hounds in a hunt, the fox escapes completely unscathed.

When a fox is snared, it may remain alive for hours, caught by the leg or the body in a loop of wire, before being dispatched when the gamekeeper inspects his snares. There is evidence of at least 40 percent wounding rates when foxes are shot, especially in the increasing practice of 'lamping': night-shooting using beams of light to reveal and dazzle the fox Poisoning of foxes, although illegal, is reported sometimes, causing slow, agonizing death. Many foxes, and other wildlife, are the victims of UK road traffic every night and day, causing death or severe wounding.

None of the above alternative means of 'control' is forced to observe a closure while foxes are breeding. In the 21st century vixens are too often shot or snared in spring when they have litters of cubs underground who then starve to death. All these alternative means of culling foxes are far less visible than traditional foxhunting, and therefore impossible to regulate. Some farming and shooting interests seek to exterminate the fox in their districts, rather than cull it, producing rural areas where nowadays foxes are hardly to be found. Instead, scavengers known as 'dustbin foxes' are far more evident in towns and cities where they are often victims of mange and traffic injuries.

Hunts have for centuries planted coverts, small woodlands and gorse patches, which foxes inhabit. In many parts of rural Britain, such as the Shires of central England, these coverts have added great beauty and diversity to the landscape, and provided habitats for many other forms of wild-life. Hunts have long encouraged traditional hedge-building, recognised as a vital part of wild-life and bird conservation in general.

Foxes still survive in our countryside since 2005, although less frequently in some areas, especially in the Midlands, than before the Hunting Act became law.

As made clear by informed veterinary opinion, since the Hunting Act the fox is far more at risk of a slow and painful death.

CHAPTER 16

PUTTING
FOXHUNTING'S CASE

They made every effort to put over their case;
And the lies against hunting they could soon efface.
They marched through the streets;
They held protests at meets;
They explained to Lord Burns
(In the hope that he learns).
They talked to MPs,
They said thank you and please –
But what e'er came to pass
'Twas all about class.

DURING the postwar years, organised foxhunting with hounds was the subject of a three-pronged attack: twisted propaganda in parts of the media, a long-running political campaign, and bullying tactics in the hunting field by self-styled Hunt Saboteurs.

It says much for the fortitude of hunting people, and their belief in the values of the sport, that in the 2012-13 season there were still 183 Foxhunts registered with the MFHA, showing no reduction since Tony Blair's Labour government enacted a Bill intended to ban hunting with hounds in February 2005. Coursing Clubs became inactive in Britain after the Bill, but Stag Hunts, Harrier and Beagle packs and Minkhounds survive. The Welsh gun-packs continue to operate.

Foxhunting has regulated itself since 1856 when Boodles Club in London set up its own Hunting Committee to arbitrate on boundary disputes, succeeded by the Masters of Foxhounds Association in 1881 (see chapter seven).

None of the arguments in favour of foxhunting were easy to convey to an increasingly urban British society in the late 20th century. Many of foxhunting's opponents, especially the political element, wilfully mixed up the hunting issue with the class war. Riders to hounds were dismissed as arrogant toffs, although it is indisputable that foxhunting people, whether mounted or on foot, have always represented a very wide section of society. It is far easier to join your local Hunt that some golf clubs.

The British Field Sports Society was formed in 1930 in response to attempts to ban staghunting by the League for the Prohibition of Cruel Sports, formed six years earlier. A small anti-hunting movement huffed and puffed in the 1930s, but immediately after the second world war its fortunes were encouraged by the new Labour government where there were some allies. A Private Members' Bill was debated in Parliament in February, 1949 to attempt abolition of staghunting and coursing. Hunting people flocked to join the BFSS which reached over 100,000 membership.

West Midlands hunting people rode through London's West End during the second reading of the Bill, forming a group which survived thereafter as the Piccadilly Hunt. Labour's Minister of Agriculture Tom Williams strongly opposed the Bill in the Commons debate, and it was defeated by 113 votes. This led to the 1951 Scott Henderson Report on hunting, which acquitted the sport of cruelty allegations.

The anti-hunting group, now called the League Against Cruel Sports, continued to attempt parliamentary action against hare coursing through Private Members' Bills during the 1960s and the 1970s. All failed, but it should have warned hunting people of trouble ahead; instead membership of the BFSS slumped alarmingly due to complacency.

A BFSS Fighting Fund was launched in 1975 to help respond to increasing threats from the LACS under a new director, Richard Course. He persuaded the Co-operative Wholesale Society to ban foxhunting on 50,000 acres of farmland which it owned. This was a major shock to the hunting world; the ban caused several Hunts, including the Fernie in Leicestershire, to curtail their fixtures. Some Labour-influenced county councils attempted to ban hunting on council-owned land, but after a long-running legal battle it was ruled against.

More threateningly, the RSPCA in 1976 declared itself opposed to all forms of hunting with hounds, becoming an ally of the LACS and the International Fund for Animal Welfare which had received huge funding during its opposition to Canadian seal hunting. IFAW and the RSPCA gave financial backing to an anti-hunting campaign in Britain, buying space for advertisements attacking hunting in the national press. Later IFAW was to donate through the charitable trust, the Political Animal Lobby, £1 million to Labour, and £4,000 to the Conservative Party's Animal Welfare Group.

The political threat continued to sharpen near the end of the century. Anti-hunting Bills were defeated in Parliament in 1992 and 1995, but the campaign work was proving a heavy commitment for the BFSS. Tony Blair, new leader of Labour in opposition, said he would give time for a free vote on hunting if Labour were in power. He won the General Election in May, 1997 with a huge majority of 172.

Hunting responded quickly: led by their charismatic new chief executive, Robin Hanbury-Tenison, the BFSS held an impressive pro-hunting rally in London's Hyde Park in July 1997. Hunting people marched from the West Country, Wales and Scotland to Hyde Park, and many more came by coach and train, producing a crowd of some 120,000. They cheered 28 pro-hunting speakers, led by the BFSS President, Labour peeress Baroness Mallalieu QC.

The rally received a good press, who noted the hunters had picked up all their litter in Hyde Park, but the anti-hunting lobby in the Labour Party was pressing for more parliamentary action. The Foster Bill against hunting in 1998 showed the result of anti-hunting propaganda by a winning a 260 majority, with 411 MPs in favour of abolition, and 151 against.

In 1998 hunting's defence broadened its base by transforming the BFSS into the Countryside Alliance. On 1 March that year the Alliance launched its first CA March through London, over 285,000 people coming to the capital on a Sunday. They paraded peacefully from the Embankment to Hyde Park, again receiving a good press. Commentators criticized Labour for creating a dangerous wedge between town and country.

Although the Foster Bill was dropped, it encouraged Blair's Labour government to introduce its own anti-hunting Bill. In response, the Countryside Alliance held enthusiastically-supported demonstrations and rallies in favour of hunting at Labour Party conferences, and in the regions.

A 'Middle Way' Group was formed in 1998 in the House of Commons from MPs of all parties who sought a compromise whereby hunting would continue under a new licensing system, run by an independent authority. The Countryside Alliance leadership, with the MFHA and other hunting organisations, rejected this option as being far too restrictive in detail. It was supported by some leading members of the Blair cabinet, including the Home Secretary Jack Straw, who said it was 'the best option hunting will get'.

The government set up the Burns Inquiry into hunting in 1999. The Alliance spent about £1 million in providing an expertly-presented case for hunting to Lord Burns and his colleagues.

Lord Burns' committee report was published in June 2000. Its tone and content could not possibly justify an overall ban, said many independent commentators. The report found that other forms of control of foxes, hares and deer involved suffering, and it could not be proved that hunting was the worst method in welfare terms.

On 1 March 2000 the Watson Bill to abolish 'hunting with dogs' in Scotland, where there were ten packs of Foxhounds, was introduced in the newly created Scottish Parliament. Incredibly in view of so many other priorities, this was the first Scottish Private Member's Bill. It was described by its opponents as class-war revenge politics, since support for a ban came from Labour's central belt of seats where old enmities against Scotland's traditional land-owning classes were still voiced. There was a protracted political and legal battle against the Bill, but it prevailed.

The Scottish Countryside Alliance held a protest march through Edinburgh in December, 2001, supported by a crowd of some 15,000 field sportsmen. The Scottish Bill is differently framed to the Hunting Act in England and Wales. In Scotland, in order to protect game shooting interests, there is less restriction on using 'dogs' to flush out quarry from coverts to be shot, and the Scottish Fox Hunts have survived within the confines of this Bill.

The Northern Ireland government has continued to resist attempts at a legal ban on hunting with hounds. So the United Kingdom is anything but united on this issue which affects so many in the countryside. Foxhunting with hounds remains legal and popular in the Irish republic, taking place also in France, Italy and Spain, throughout North America, and in Australia. Foxes do not inhabit New Zealand, but hare hunting with hounds is popular.

Foxhunting with hounds survived to the end of the 20th century in Britain, despite increasing opposition from animal rights groups, using press and broadcasting to distribute their message to the public and politicians.

After the Burns committee findings, many believed an all-out ban would not be attempted in the House of Commons, even by a Labour government. But the early 21st century was to test the resolve and courage of hunting people to the ultimate.

CHAPTER 17

THE CHALLENGE OF THE HUNTING ACT

Trudging along its weary way,
The Hunting Bill was terribly battered;
All common sense completely scattered.
And at the end of this wearisome farce –
The unspeakable Act fell flat on its arse.

IN 2001, for the first time ever, a government Bill to 'deal with' hunting in England and Wales was introduced. Historically, there had been 22 attempts in Parliament to ban hunting through Private Members' Bills.

Many independent commentators condemned Labour for giving priority to hunting when the government was faced with compelling issues such as Britain's failing economy, terrorism, public health and education. Parliament devoted 700 hours of expensive time to the hunting issue at enormous cost to the taxpayer.

Alun Michael, a junior DEFRA minister with well known anti-hunting views, was given the poisoned chalice of handling the new Bill for Labour. On many occasions when he appeared in the countryside he faced angry protests from hunting people.

Hunts across England and Wales held mass meets in protest, and the Countryside Alliance planned a second march in London for 18 March 2001. But early in February Britain's stock farming was hit by a catastrophic outbreak of foot and mouth disease which lasted most of the year, and the march was postponed. On 26 March the House of Lords voted for the continuance of hunting by voluntary self-regulation by a majority of 141.

The Lords rejected the Middle Way proposal for government licensing, and decisively voted against an outright ban, by 249 votes. Some observers criticized pro-hunting peers for voting against the Middle Way 'solution' which appeared the only one the Labour government might accept. The pro-hunters in the Lords were reluctant to abandon coursing and staghunting which would have been banned outright under the Middle Way solution, and they feared an over-restrictive form of government licensing under Labour.

The June 2001 General Election meant the Bill ran out of time, but after another Labour victory to regain power with a majority of 166, the hunting issue erupted again – this time in the House of Commons in March 2002. On a free vote, with Labour's majority taking its toll, the Commons overwhelmingly supported a hunting ban, by a 211 majority. The House, dominated by the large Labour majority, rejected the Middle Way and self-regulation decisively.

Next day the House of Lords changed its stance of the previous year – and voted in favour of the Middle Way proposal, by a 307 majority. Lord Mancroft, the hunting peer on the Countryside Alliance board, admitted there were 'considerable risks' in going down the Middle Way path, and said they would not throw away staghunting and coursing as a price.

The House of Lords and the House of Commons were now on a collision path on the hunting issue. This did not bother Labour

MPs because they were keen to reform, if not abolish, the House of Lords. Once again hunting was mixed up in battles which had far more to do with cross-party strife than wild animal welfare.

Lord Donoughue, a former Labour minister, wrote 'it is politically crazy that a Labour government with a massive future legislative programme....should waste valuable political energy on such a marginal and divisive issue'.

The Countryside Alliance continued to run a series of protests, but strove to prevent hunting people carrying out threats such as blocking motor-ways with tractors, warning that causing major inconvenience to the general public would do immense harm to the hunting cause.

DEFRA ran a consultation process on hunting in Whitehall in September 2002 when the familiar arguments were churned out again by both sides. On the 22nd of that month the postponed second Countryside Alliance March in London took place with the largest attendance yet – 407,791 people forming a truly impressive procession on foot from the City of London and south of the Thames to finish in Parliament Square. It was entirely law-abiding; police on duty were not called upon to take action.

It was wryly noted that the Countryside March contrasted starkly with law breaking protests such as the Poll Tax riots in central London which had been followed by the hated legislation being abandoned. Leading American foxhunters flew to London to take part in this Liberty and Livelihood March, waving the Stars and Stripes and pro-hunting banners. Youth was well represented: one cheerful group of girls carried a banner proclaiming 'Hunting is Better than Sex'.

On December 2001 Alun Michael announced a second Hunting Bill which would ban hare coursing and deer hunting, but would allow foxhunting under licence. There would be tight controls including a 'cruelty test' and a 'utility test' which sought to prevent Hunts damaging livestock and crops. Since hunting had survived for hundreds of years by hunting on other people's land with their permission, the utility clause was irrelevant.

Pro-hunters and anti-hunters hated the government's Bill; it was described as a 'silly fudge' in the press. Labour MP Gerald Kaufman, a virulent anti-hunting campaigner, described it as 'botched' and declared he would settle for nothing less than a complete ban on hunting with hounds.

On 16 December Parliament Square saw police grappling with some hunting people outside the House of Commons. They had separated from a Countryside March from Hyde Park, heading for its headquarters on the south side of the Thames. Police blocked Westminster Bridge to try to prevent pro-hunters crossing back to Parliament Square, but many broke through. Some chained themselves to Parliament's railings; a handful threw fireworks. At last it seemed an angry countryside protest had erupted in the heart of Westminster. There were traffic hold-ups and Westminster Underground Station was closed. A Countryside Alliance official climbed on to a bus to urge protestors to go home, but many remained.

Inside the Commons the second reading of the government Bill was foundering under opposition from Labour's back-bench MPs. In January the following year, 2003, Alun Michael agreed to amend the Bill to limit foxhunting to pest control.

Yet again the anti-hunters were frustrated: the Iraq War erupted in April 2003, and it was blatantly ludicrous for MPs to spend time debating foxhunting. Yet, later in the year the Hunting Bill tottered on through the Commons, with more humiliating scenes for Alun Michael who was verbally lashed by Labour MPs calling for a complete ban instead of his so-called compromise.

Eventually Alun Michael, after consulting cabinet colleagues, amended the Bill to a complete ban, and it was passed by an overwhelming majority of 208. Prime Minister Tony Blair was notable by his absence from the Commons during this debate.

The Alliance published an NOP poll showing that 99 percent of Labour supporters thought there were more important issues for government than tackling hunting. The political game seemed far from being lost for hunting.

The House of Lords strongly opposed the government Bill and overturned it in the committee stage, instead voting for a system of regulated foxhunting. This latest folly by Labour was allowed to expire in the autumn of 2003.

Sure enough, in the spring of 2004 Labour tried again, reintroducing its Hunting Bill which this time would ban coursing, but would give foxhunting, deer, hare, and mink hunting a two year reprieve until 2006, affording the Hunts time to wind down, said Alun Michael. Clearly he expected the collapse of all Hunts which indicated his lack of knowledge about rural Britain's own priorities.

This was widely dismissed as an attempt to defer the hunting battle until after the next General Election expected in May 2005. At last the fourth government Bill to ban hunting, much amended in form, was debated in the House of Commons on 15 September 2004.

Although public demonstrations are normally forbidden in Parliament Square while the House is sitting, some 20,000 hunting people packed the Square during the debate, waving banners, and listening to rousing speeches from a temporary platform erected by the Countryside Alliance.

Hundreds of police in riot gear stood shoulder-to-shoulder behind barriers in front of the Palace of Westminster. Occasional fireworks were let off in the crowd, and scuffles erupted between police and some protestors at the barriers. Police wielded batons, and 16 people were injured, including some women who claimed they had been beaten by police 'when all we wanted was to sit down and sing'. Lurid colour photographs appeared in the press next day depicting hunting protestors with bloodied head injuries.

Inside the House of Commons a unique drama was unfolding. Eight pro-hunting protestors disguised themselves as building workers, and with astonishing ease five of them made their way on to the floor of the House during the hunting debate. Their leader,

Otis Ferry, Joint Master and huntsman of the South Shropshire, put a hand on the mace and shouted at the Labour front bench: 'You are a disgrace'.

The bold intruders were escorted out, and the debate was temporarily suspended for 18 minutes. The debate resumed with the Conservative rural spokesman, James Gray, attacking the Hunting Bill as 'a constitutional scandal of the worse kind... an intolerant, ignorant and prejudiced Bill... an affront to liberal democracy... the people of the countryside will neither tolerate nor forget it...'

Labour's DEFRA Minister, Eliot Morley, wound up the debate for the government. He declared it was 'not always rational to take into account minority views', and the sport deserved to be banned.

Mr Morley, whose Parliamentary career was to end in 2011 with a 16 month jail sentence for dishonestly claiming more than £30,000 in expenses, declared hunting was a 'moral issue'.

Otis Ferry and his seven pro-hunting companions were kept overnight in police custody, and later each was sentenced to an 18 months conditional discharge for a public order offence. There was a huge Parliamentary row over the lack of security enabling the first invasion of the Commons in session since Cromwell and his troops had marched in, 351 years earlier.

Two months later on 17 November 2004, the House of Lords made massive changes to the Hunting Act, restoring licensed hunting, and inserting a three year implementation process.

Next day, amid parliamentary scenes of confusion and chaos, the Bill was shuttled back and for the between the two Houses. Alun Michael's attempts to delay the ban until 2007 was heavily defeated. *The Times* writer Ann Trenneman commented: 'Democracy was lurching around like a drunk at closing time...'

Tony Blair was absent again from the House of Commons during the hunting debate, and therefore did not vote. Much later he went on the record as saying he felt the Hunting Act had been a mistake.

At 9pm the Speaker of the House of Commons, Michael Martin, amid cries of 'shame!' announced the Hunting Bill, amended by MPs to be a ban, would become law under the provisions of the Parliament Act which asserts the supremacy of the Commons over the Lords. This was a highly controversial move by the government, since the original Parliament Act in 1911 was brought in to aid government push through finance Bills.

But the Countryside Alliance's legal challenge against use of the Parliament Act to ram through the Hunting Act was rejected by a committee of nine law lords in October 2005. Nor was an appeal to the European Court of Human Rights to be successful.

Hunting with hounds in England and Wales, after centuries as an accepted and popular pastime in the countryside, was given merely three months to prepare for a legal ban. The Act came into force on 18 February, well before the end of a normal hunting season.

Hunts each held their last day of traditional hunting just before that date, many fearing this would be the demise of the sport in any form. Gloating comments published from some elements in the anti-hunting lobby clearly betrayed their priority in 'defeating the toffs'.

There were sad faces, and some tears, among hunting people attending the 'last meets', but there was also defiance, and a determination to maintain the Hunts as an invaluable part of rural life. Masters and Hunt Committees wanted to see what could be achieved in the following season, 2005-6, under the terms of the ludicrous legislation. Already the Bill was widely criticised in the press as very badly drawn up, and open to ridicule as being grossly inconsistent.

The Countryside Alliance vowed immediately to pursue a fight for repeal. But in February 2005 when Labour's ban became law, there were few who would have confidently predicted that, far from winding down, all Hunts affected by the ban would survive, with ample support, for many a season to come.

CHAPTER 18

FOXHUNTING – THE FUTURE

Hark! The sound of voice and horn
Stirs the heart on a hunting morn.
Youth at the meet tightens its girth,
Then rides with joy o'er our precious earth,
Learning anew the ways of the Chase
That still beguile our island race.

'TALLY HO! The ban's still there – but so are they.'

This was the heading in *The Independent* newspaper over a report on the 2012 Boxing Day meets of hunts throughout the country. It summed up the survival of Britain's packs of hounds since the Hunting Act was enforced seven years earlier, and the remarkable support the Hunts are still receiving in the countryside.

Instead, the usual lists of meets have appeared each season since 2005, with hounds going out at least twice a week from each Hunt kennels, larger packs managing three to four days per week.

The crucial element in hunting's survival since 2005 has been the willingness of most farmers and landowners to continue to allow hounds on their land despite the Act. It would not have been possible for the Hunts to survive after the Hunting Act was enforced in February 2005, if they had been permanently barred from privately owned land throughout England and Wales.

Their continued welcome from farmers and landowners was maintained despite the Hunting Act's attempt to deter them with a clause making it an offence to permit land to be used for hunting.

The Hunting Act created the offences of 'hunting a wild mammal with a dog', and all forms of hare-coursing.

The Labour government which drew up the Act was in a major quandary because the above offences could also curtail shooting as a sport, because dogs are used in these activities for flushing quarry to the guns, in locating game and retrieving after shooting.

So the Bill allows a number of exemptions which involve patently ridiculous anomalies. Under the Act it is legal to hunt rats and rabbits with dogs, but not foxes, deer, or hares. Doubtless if men wore red coats and rode horses in pursuit of hounds hunting rats and rabbits these activities would have been banned as well – judging by the abusive rhetoric employed by the anti-hunters during their campaign.

Under the Hunting Act hounds may be used to flush out wild animals from coverts if they are to be shot. Terriers can be used below ground to flush out foxes to be shot in protection of game birds reared for shooting. This provision caused much derision because it does not refer to protecting farm stock, such as lambs, which can be a prey for foxes.

Dogs, which includes hounds of course, may be used to retrieve shot hares which have been injured, an exemption used by Harrier and Beagle Packs since the Act. Picking up after shooting demonstrates that hares and other mammals are frequently not killed outright by shooting, and that quick retrieval is vital for humane dispatch of the injured animal.

The Act allows flushing of a 'wild mammal' from cover (hunting uses the word covert) 'to enable it to be hunted by a bird of prey'. This exemption has been used by some Fox Hunts who are accompanied by falconers carrying birds of prey.

Since 2005 Britain's registered Fox Hunts have operated within the above exemptions, and hounds have hunted artificially-laid trails across country, which is a form of drag hunting. The trail is often laid by a rider dragging a scented rag on the end of a rope.

'It is immensely encouraging that seven years on from the ban, Hunts are in good heart, 'said the Countryside Alliance executive chairman Barney White-Spunner at the end of 2012.

He cited a survey of over 120 Hunts by the Alliance which showed that most Hunts, over 85 percent, still assisted farmers and other land managers by culling foxes; over 83 percent of Hunts carried out the same amount of hunting as they did before the ban; and over 60 percent felt better supported by their local community.

The survey showed that 56.7 percent of Hunts thought they had the same number of subscribers, 30 percent believed they had more, and over 27 percent of hunt supporters' clubs had increased in size. Over 85 percent of Hunts were still offering a fox control service for farmers.

Whatever the estimates of hound hunting's survival, the Alliance was still firmly pledged to repeal of the Hunting Act. Barney White-Spunner said in his 2012 New Year's message it was clear there was a 'down side' through the 'immense difficulties the law has brought for Hunts', and it had brought no benefit for the quarry species.

The Masters of Foxhounds Association was much concerned that in the long term the limitations of the Act, and associated pressures and harassment by vigilantes, are seriously detrimental to Fox Hunts. These factors, it was feared, would make it increasingly difficult for Hunts to recruit staff, to attract and maintain competent Masters, and in a few cases it could make access to land more difficult.

By 2012 some of the celebrated packs of Foxhounds in the Midlands and elsewhere were experiencing falling incomes due to loss of full subscriptions, as opposed to visitors paying caps for a day's hunting. Apart from the Hunting Act, other factors were already hitting foxhunting in the Shires countries in the heart of England which traditionally attracted hundreds of non-resident subscribers. These Hunts were suffering from reduced hunting country through increasing urbanisation, and the march of plough over former grassland. Hunts in the Shires which were attended by mounted fields of 150 or more at their most popular fixtures, were seeing fields of well under 100, with far fewer riders bringing second horses, so that mounted fields dwindled sharply before hounds had ceased hunting.

Between 2005 and 2010, according to the Ministry of Justice, 332 people were prosecuted under the Hunting Act, and 129 were found guilty. A mere eight of the convictions involved hunt staff. Most of the prosecutions were for minor offences, such as poaching hares or deer, or ratting or rabbiting without the landowner's permission.

Up to the end of 2012 there were nine attempts to prosecute staff of Fox Hunts under the Act and six of them failed. The first successful prosecution was brought against the Exmoor huntsman Tony Wright, but it was overturned in Exeter Crown Court where his defence that he was using a couple of hounds to flush a fox to be shot – an exemption under the Act – was accepted.

When it was formed in 2010, the Conservative-Liberal Democrat coalition government promised a free vote on whether the Hunting Act should be repealed. Prime Minister David Cameron said: 'It has not been a demonstrable success, and is difficult to enforce. It is an unnecessary drain on police resources, and there have been few prosecutions. Only three Hunts have been successfully prosecuted for illegal hunting'.

Increasing numbers of anti-hunting activists using long range cameras were in the countryside to obtain photographic 'evidence' that hounds had actually chased a fox during a hunting day. Prosecutions were privately carried out by animal rights organizations.

In 2012 hunt staff, and some Masters, were fined after conviction of alleged offences under the Act at the Crawley and Horsham, Fernie, Meynell and South Staffs, and the Heythrop. The Heythrop case revealed to the public just how much money and time and the animal rights lobby was spending in trying to achieve hunting prosecutions.

The RSPCA spent about £330,000 in pursuing the prosecution of the Heythrop, and the District Judge commented that this was a 'quite staggering' figure, remarking 'members of the public may feel that RSPCA funds can be more usefully employed'. These remarks were quoted in the press.

The RSPCA was widely criticized for spending so much on a hunting case involving the use of 500 hours of film footage of the Hunt, and highly expensive legal representation. Frequent references in the press to the Heythrop hunting country being in the constituency of the Prime Minister led to accusations that the prosecution was politically motivated. There were complaints to the Charity Commission that the RSPCA had breached charity regulations. All this was denied by the RSPCA which spoke of launching a 'crusade' against people it deemed 'wildlife criminals'.

The Daily Telegraph declared in a leader on 26 December, 2012:

'The explanation for using such an enormous sum of money from charitable donations on this prosecution was unconvincing... The fact that country people have adapted to the new law in a way that allows them to continue hunting within fairly rigorous guidelines is apparently anathema to the charity, and it intends to hunt the hunters.
'This stance will no doubt help recruit new, and younger, members and their donations. But many others who instinctively support the RSPCA and its work will find this

attempt to criminalise country people for a pursuit that has been part of the fabric of rural life for centuries deeply regrettable.'

Despite the politics, and the posturing of the anti-hunting lobby, Britain's Fox Hunts have continued since the Hunting Act to make their unique contribution to the quality of life in the country-side. Many retired people spend hours each season following Fox Hunts by car, on bicycles, or on foot.

Point-to-points, Hunt dances, quiz evenings and a host of other social functions have continued to bring much pleasure and community spirit to the countryside. As well as augmenting their funds, Hunts regularly donate money to local and national charities.

Pony Clubs associated with the Hunts support special children's meets in the holidays with huge enthusiasm and enjoyment. Each new generation brings eager recruits to the hunting field.

The annual puppy shows held at Hunt Kennels are still well attended by puppy walkers and many others showing the keenest interest in the breeding and development of one of the most perfectly conserved of working animals – the Foxhound. Peterborough's annual Festival of Hunting at the East of England Showground is supported by hundreds of enthusiasts coming to see all varieties of the hunting hound on show. Peterborough Royal Foxhound Show remains a main focus of the Festival.

The history of foxhunting in Britain is far from over.

We salute all who have made this possible, and to the many who will still be following Foxhounds in the future, we bestow the time-honoured message – Good Hunting!

Alastair Jackson & Michael Clayton

GLOSSARY OF HUNTING TERMS

(*Note*: Many of these terms refer only to traditional foxhunting practice before the Hunting Act 2004 – *see* Chapter 17)

All On: An expression used by the Whipper-in to inform the Huntsman that all hounds in the pack are present.

Amateur Huntsman: An unpaid huntsman who directs the hounds on a hunting day.

At Fault: When hounds have lost the scent during the hunt.

Babbler: A hound which bays or 'gives tongue' when it has not picked up a scent, and may mislead the huntsman and the pack; considered a fault.

Bag Fox: An obsolete practice of loosing a fox from a bag for hounds to hunt, strictly forbidden by the Master of Foxhounds Association since it was founded in 1881.

Benches: Traditionally the wooden platforms on which hounds sleep in Hunt Kennels. Nowadays made of insulated smooth concrete and covered with straw or shavings.

Blind: A 'blind' ditch is one covered in summer growth. The country is 'blind' in the autumn.

Billet: A fox's droppings.

Blank: A covert is 'blank' when it does not contain a fox, or a 'blank day' is a day's hunting when no foxes are found.

Blowing Away: The exciting call on the horn blown by the huntsman when the hounds move away from a covert.

Blowing Out: A longer, less exuberant note, blown by the huntsman to call out of a covert where there is no fox (a blank cover).

Bob-Tailed: A bob-tailed fox has little or no tail or 'brush'.

Bolt: To bolt a fox is to drive it above ground from an earth or drain, often using a terrier.

Bottom: A deep gully or ravine, which cannot be jumped or thick impenetrable undergrowth in a covert.

Brace: Foxes are counted in braces, two to a brace, e.g. three foxes is one-and-a-half brace.

Break: When a fox runs from a covert into the open.

Break-Up: When a fox is killed by hounds , and subsequently consumed by the pack.

Brush: The fox's tail.

Bullfinch: A high hedge with spreading top which a horse has to jump through.

Burst: The first part of a run if hound are running fast.

Butcher Boots: Plain long, black riding boots without 'tops'.

Button: Each Hunt has its own coat button (either black or brass) with a unique design. Traditionally Masters awarded the Hunt Button as an honour to supportive mounted subscribers.

Bye-Day: An extra day's hunting to that scheduled for the season.

Cap: A peaked cap covered in black velvet, traditionally worn by the Masters, huntsman, and whippers-in, with the ribbons down at the back. Many followers nowadays wear caps, some with chinstraps and modern insulation, but hunting etiquette requires mounted followers to sew the ribbons into the cap.

Cap: Also refers to the fee paid for one day's hunting by a visitor not paying the Hunt's full subscription.

Carries a Scent: Meaning the ground surface is holding the scent of the fox, usually dependent on air temperature and other factors. May be a 'poor scent' in unhelpful conditions, which limits the hunting ability by the hounds.

Carry the Horn: To be the huntsman.

Carry: Mud or other sticky substance, which adheres to the fox's and hounds' pads and paws.

Cast: Hounds spreading out in search of a lost scent. A huntsman may 'cast' his hounds to recover a lost scent by encouraging them to spread where he thinks the line of scent is lying.

Challenge: The hound which ' gives tongue' on finding the scent of a fox is said to 'open' or 'challenge'.

Charlie: A nickname name for the fox, reputed to be after Charles James Fox, the tempestuous 19th Century Whig politician.

Check: Temporary or permanent loss by hounds of the fox's scent.

Chop: To kill a fox before it has time to run.

Clean Ground: Land which is free of distracting scents.

Cold Line: An old line of scent left many minutes or hours previously by the fox.

Cold Scenting Country: Land which does not readily hold scent.

Country: The hunting territory of each Hunt, with boundaries other Hunts must observe; different parts of a 'Hunt country' may be hunted on particular days of the week.

Couple: Hounds are counted in couples (traditionally hounds were sometimes 'coupled' to an older hound while on exercise by a collar and chain). Odd numbers are referred to as halves, e.g. seven hounds is 'three-and-a-half couple'

Course: The pursuit of a fox while it is well within the view of hounds. To course a fox is to hunt it by sight, compared with normal hunting by scent.

Covert *(pronounced Cover):* An area where foxes dwell: wooded or covered in gorse or thicket.

Cry: The sound made by the hounds when hunting.

Cub: A young fox.

Cubhunting: Autumn hunting before the opening meet at the end of October. Provided an opportunity to train young hounds only to hunt foxes, and to cull and disperse the fox population.

Cur dog: In the hunting field any other dog which is not a foxhound.

Dog Fox: A male fox.

Double: A fence, or a bank, with ditches on both sides. Or the huntsman 'doubles' his horn when blowing a succession of quick staccato notes when he needs hounds in a hurry.

Draft: Hounds transferred to another pack.

Drag Line: An artificial scent laid by man, which hounds follow in 'drag hunting'.

Drag: The scent left by a fox after its own night's hunting. Or an artificial line of scent.

Draw: To draw a covert is to send hounds in to seek a fox. Or 'The draw' is the day's order of coverts to be drawn. Or 'To draw a hound' is to call an individual hound from the pack.

Earth: The earth is the fox's underground home.

Enter: The introduction of young hound to foxhunting.

Feather: A hound 'feathers' when it is following a faint line. It waves its stern and keeps its nose to the ground, but does not speak.

Feathers: The long hairs on the lower end of a hound's stern.

Fence Mender: The fence mender follows the Hunt in a vehicle and repairs any damage caused by the horses.

Field Master: Either a Master, or appointed by the Masters, the Field Master leads the mounted followers across country.

Field: The mounted followers are known as The Field.

Fly fences: Fences which can be cleared at a gallop.

Foil: A smell which obscures that of the fox's scent. Or a fox which doubles back is said to be 'running his foil'.

Given Best: The fox is 'given best' when it has eluded the hounds, and the huntsman decides not to pursue is further.

Going: Ground conditions e.g. hard, heavy, deep (soft), wet or good.

Good Head: Hounds 'carry a good head' if they run well together and are not strung out.

Gone Away: *See* 'Blowing Away'.

Gone to Ground: When a fox takes refuge in an earth or drain.

Guarantee: An annually fixed sum of money given by the Committee to the Master to meet the costs of running and maintaining the Hunt, which includes salaries of hunt staff, stables and kennels.

Hack On: To ride a horse to a meet.

Hairy: A poorly maintained or overgrown hedge, which is difficult to jump.

Hark Forward *(pronounced 'Hark For-or-orrad')*: The huntsman's shout if a fox has been seen further on, or hounds have found the line of the fox.

Head: To 'head' the fox is to interfere with its direction, causing it to veer or run back.

Heads Up: Hounds lifting their heads up from the scent showing a lack of perseverance.

Heel: If hounds encounter the line of scent of the fox at the wrong angle, they may pursue the scent in the opposite direction to which the fox is running, running 'heel line'.

Hit The Line: When a hound finds and follows the scent of the fox he is 'hitting the line'.

Hold Up: To surround a covert and attempt to prevent foxes leaving, usually during autumn hunting.

Holloa (*pronounced 'Holler'*): The shout by a person who sees a fox, informing huntsman and hounds.

Huic Holloa (*pronounced 'Hike Holler'*): A shout drawing the attention of Huntsman and hounds to a Holloa by another person at a further distance.

Huntsman: The key figure in hunting. Either a professional, or an amateur who is usually a Master. Practices the science of venery in guiding hounds in the hunting field, and supervises their breeding and care in Kennels.

Kennel Huntsman: A professional member of Hunt staff who looks after the kennels and hounds, when the hounds are hunted by an amateur. A professional huntsman is his own kennel-huntsman.

Larking: Jumping fences unnecessarily when hounds are not running.

Lay On: When the huntsman puts his hounds on a scent.

Lift: A huntsman may 'lift' hounds to a point where he thinks the fox has gone.

Make: 'Making' the pack is counting it.

Mark: Hounds mark ('give tongue') at the mouth of an earth or drain where the fox is underground.

Meet: The predetermined location where the Master of the hunt will be joined by the hounds, huntsman and the Field in preparation for hunting.

Mixed Pack: Comprises both dog and bitch hounds.

Music: Commonly describes the cry of the hounds.

Mute: Hounds which will not 'speak' when following a scent, considered a serious fault.

Nose: Refers to the ability of a hound to pick up and follow a scent.

Open: When a hound 'speaks', or 'gives tongue' on finding a scent.

Opening-Meet: First formal meet of the season, around 1 November, which will follow autumn hunting.

Over Riding: Follower riding among the hounds, much frowned upon.

Own the Line: The first hound to 'Speak' on detecting a line of scent.

Oxer: Thorn fence with rail on one side. Or a double oxer, a fence with rail on both sides.

Pad: Fox's foot.

Pink: 'Hunting pink' refers to 'pink coats', but traditionalists insisted Hunt coats should only be referred to as red or scarlet. 'Pink' merely referred to a London tailor who made Hunt coats.

Pink tops: Refers to a white-pink colour of the boot tops used by fashionable foxhunters with white breeches. Nowadays mahogany coloured tops are the prevailing fashion.

Point: The distance in a straight line between the start and the furthest distance reached in the route of a run, e.g. 'a five mile point', although fox, hounds and followers will have run much further than five miles before the run is finished.

Quick Thing: A very fast, short run.

Rasper: A formidable fence.

Rat Catcher: Riding outfit worn by Masters and followers, but not the huntsman and whippers-in, during autumn hunting, ideally comprising tweed coat, bowler hat, brown breeches and brown or black boots. Occasionally worn by individuals during the season.

Rate: To rate a hound is to reprimand it.

Ringing: When a fox tends to run in circular routes.

Riot: When a foxhound pursues a quarry other than a fox.

Scent: Smell of the hunted animal. Strength of scent varies considerably.

Shire Pack: Nineteenth century definition of the 'fashionable' packs hunting wholly or partly in Leicestershire and Rutland, e.g. Quorn, Belvoir, Cottesmore, Fernie, Pytchley.

Speak: Hounds 'speak', 'give tongue' or 'bay'; it is not called barking!

Skirter: A hound which cuts corners instead of following the line of scent of the fox; considered a fault.

Stain: The scent of other animals which masks that of the quarry.

Stale Line: The old scent of a fox.

Stern: A hound's tail.

Stopping: Temporarily blocking a fox's earth.

Stub Bred: Foxes bred above earth.

Tail Hounds: Hounds at the end of the pack when they are running.

Tally Ho Back: A shout that the fox is seen doubling back into the covert.

Tally Ho: A shout by someone who has seen the fox. Facing the direction in which the fox travelled and holding the hat in the air will assist the huntsman.

Throw their tongues: Hounds 'throw their tongues' when they 'speak' to the line of the fox.

Top Boots: Long black leather boots with contrasting coloured top, nowadays mahogany-coloured.

Trencher Fed: Old system whereby hounds were kept privately and brought together as a pack on a hunting day.

Unentered: A young hound, which has not started hunting with the pack.

View: The sighting of the fox.

Walk: Weaned hound puppies kennelled with volunteers, named 'Puppy Walkers', until returned to the pack before their entry to hunting.

Ware! *(pronounced 'war')*: Shout to warn of danger, e.g. 'Ware wire!' (Beware, wire in a fence you might be jumping!)

Whelp: Unweaned hound puppy.

Whipper-in: Assistant to the huntsman in controlling hounds.

MFHA-Recognised Hunts in the UK and North America

Grove & Rufford
Hampshire (HH)
Haydon
Herefordshire, North
Herefordshire, South
Heythrop
High Peak
Holcombe
Holderness
Hursley Hambledon
Hurworth
Irfon & Towy
Isle of Wight
Jed Forest
Kent, East with West Street
Kimblewick
Kincardineshire
Lamerton
Lanarkshire & Renfrewshire
Lauderdale
Ledbury
Ledbury, North
Liddesdale
Llandeilo Farmers
Llangeinor
Llanwnnen Farmers
Ludlow
Mendip Farmers
Meynell & South Staffordshire
Middleton
Minehead
Monmouthshire
Morpeth
New Forest
Norfolk, West
Notts, South
Oakley
Old Surrey Burstow & West Kent
Pembrokeshire
Pembrokeshire, South
Pendle, Forest & Craven
Pennine
Pennine, North
Pentyrch Hunt Club
Percy

Percy, West
Portman
Puckeridge
Pytchley
Quorn
Radnor & West Hereford
Royal Artillery
Saltersgate Farmers
Seavington
Sennybridge Farmers
Shropshire, North
Shropshire, South
Silverton
Sinnington
Somerset, Vale West
Somerset, West
Southdown & Eridge
South Wold
Spooners & West Dartmoor
Staffordshire, Moorland
Staffordshire, North
Staintondale
Stevenstone
Strathappin
Suffolk
Surrey Union
East Sussex & Romney Marsh
Tanatside
Taunton Vale
Tedworth
Teme Valley
Tetcott
Tetcott, South
Thurlow
Tiverton
Tivyside
Torrington Farmers
Tredegar Farmers
Tynedale
Tyne, North
United
Vale of Clettwr
VWH
Vine & Craven
Warwickshire

Sir Watkin Williams-Wynn's
Waveney
West of Yore
Western
Wheatland
Wilton
Wilts, South & West
Woodland Pytchley
Worcestershire
York & Ainsty, North
York & Ainsty, South
Ystrad Taf Fechan
Zetland

Hunts in North America

Aiken Hounds
Amwell Valley Hounds
Andrews Bridge Foxhounds
Annapolis Valley Hunt
Arapahoe Hunt
Battle Creek Hunt
Bear Creek Hounds
Beaufort Hunt
Beaver Meadow Foxhounds
Bedford County Hunt
Belle Meade Hunt
Bijou Springs Hunt
Blue Mountain Hunt
Blue Ridge Hunt
Brazos Valley Hounds
Bridlespur Hunt
Bull Run Hunt
Camargo Hunt
Camden Hunt
Caroline Hunt
Casanova Hunt
Caza Ladron
Chagrin Valley Hunt
Chula Homa Hunt
Cloudline Hounds
Commonwealth Foxhounds
De La Brooke Foxhounds
Deep Run Hunt
Edisto River Hounds

Eglinton & Caledon Hunt
Elkridge-Harford Hunt
Essex Fox Hounds
Fairfield County Hounds
Farmington Hunt
Fort Carson Hounds
Fort Leavenworth Hunt
Four Winds Foxhounds
Fox River Valley Hunt
Fraser Valley Hunt
Full Cry Hounds
Genesee Valley Hunt
Glenmore Hunt
Golden's Bridge Hounds
Goshen Hounds
Grand Canyon Hounds
Grand River Hunt
Green Creek Hounds
Green Mountain Hounds
Green Spring Valley Hounds
Guilford Hounds
Hamilton Hunt
Hard Away Whitworth Hounds
Harvard Fox Hounds
Hickory Creek Hunt
High Country Hounds
Hillsboro Hounds
Howard County – Iron Bridge Hounds
Huntingdon Valley Hunt
Independence Foxhounds
Iroquois Hunt
Juan Tomas Hounds
Kenada Fox Hounds
Keswick Hunt
Lake of Two Mountains Hunt
Limestone Creek Hunt
Live Oak Hounds
London Hunt
Long Lake Hounds
Long Run Hounds
Longacre Hunt
Longreen Foxhounds
Los Altos Hounds
Loudoun Fairfax Hunt, Inc
Loudoun Hunt

Lowcountry Hunt
Marlborough Hunt
Massbach Hounds
Mecklenburg Hounds
Mells Fox Hounds
Metamora Hunt
Miami Valley Hunt
Middlebrook Hounds
Middleburg Hunt
Middleton Place Hounds
Midland Fox Hounds
Mill Creek Hunt
Millbrook Hunt
Mission Valley Hunt Club
Misty Morning Hounds
Misty River Hounds
Moingona Hunt
Monmouth County Hunt
Montreal Hunt
Moore County Hounds
Mooreland Hunt
Mr. Jackson's Flat Creek Hounds
Mr. Stewart's Cheshire Foxhounds
Myopia Hunt
New Market – Middletown Valley
    Hounds
Nodaway River Hounds
Norfolk Hunt
North Country Hounds
North Hills Hunt
Oak Grove Hunt
Oak Ridge Fox Hunt
Old Chatham Hunt
Old Dominion Hounds
Old North Bridge Hounds
Orange County Hounds
Ottawa Valley Hunt
Palm Beach Hounds
Pickering Hunt
Piedmont Fox Hounds
Potomac Hunt
Princess Anne Hunt
Radnor Hunt
Rappahannock Hunt

Red Mountain Foxhounds
Red Rock Hounds
Reedy Creek Hounds
River Hills Foxhounds
River to River Hounds
Rockbridge Hunt
Rocky Fork Headley Hunt
Rolling Rock Hunt
Rombout Hunt
Rose Tree Foxhunting Club
Santa Fe West Hills Hunt
Santa Ynez Valley Hounds
Saxonburg Hunt
Sedgefield Hunt
Sewickley Hunt
Shakerag Hounds
Shawnee Hounds
Smithtown Hunt
South Creek Foxhounds
Spring Valley Hounds
Stonewall Hounds
Tanheath Hunt
Tejon Hounds
Tennessee Valley Hunt
Thornton Hill Fort Valley Hounds
Toronto & North York Hunt
Traders Point Hunt
Treasure State Hunt
Tryon Hounds
Warrenton Hunt
Waterloo Hunt
Wayne-DuPage Hunt
Wellington Waterloo Hunt
Wentworth Hunt Club
Whiskey Road Foxhounds
Why Worry Hounds
Wicomico Hunt
Windy Hollow Hunt
Woodbrook Hunt
Woodbury Litchfield Hills Foxhounds
Woodford Hounds
Woody Creek Hounds
Yadkin Valley Hounds